CONFESSIONS OF A PART-TIME CALL GIRL

Hi! This is Barbara.
Do you want to see me tonight?

Her clients call her Barbara. She never gives out her phone number. She chooses the men she wants. She thoroughly enjoys what she does . . . and gets paid thousands of dollars a year tax free for doing it.

She'll tell you how she got started. Her first experience as a pro. And in startlingly explicit terms, just what men want her to do. From her early straight days to a whirlwind of erotic encounters, Barbara opens up her double life, revealing all the uninhibited secrets of sex-for-hire in a wild romp of a read . . . intimate, shocking, and simply sensational!

CONFESSIONS OF A PART-TIME CALL GIRL

Barbara Ignoto

ARROW

Arrow Books Limited
20 Vauxhall Bridge Road, London SW1V 2SA

An imprint of Random House UK Limited

London Melbourne Sydney Auckland
Johannesburg and agencies throughout
the world

First published in Great Britain 1986

7 9 10 8 6

© Barbara Ignoto 1986

Printed and bound in Great Britain by
Cox & Wyman Ltd, Reading, Berkshire

ISBN 0 09 948000 X

For Steven,
who knew,
and Michael,
who didn't.

CONTENTS

I. The Life   9

II. Getting Started   16

III. The Men   38

IV. Unnatural Acts   89

V. Leading a Double Life   143

VI. Private Loves   164

VII. The Future   185

I. The Life

I'm a young woman in New York, and I work as a secretary. There are thousands like me, and if you live in New York or come here on business you've seen us—on the subways, in luncheonettes and coffee shops, in our offices looking bright and efficient and businesslike.

But there's something different about me.

I have a second job—the best part-time job in the world. Three or four nights a week I have sex for money.

I'm a part-time call girl, but I don't think of myself as a prostitute or a hooker. I think of myself as a straight person who supplements her income. And I *am* a straight person. I am basically just like all those other young middle-class women, with the same outlook on life and the same decencies. I keep my second life absolutely secret and absolutely separate from my main life. This is mainly out of necessity, of course, so I don't lose my job or get arrested, but it's also so I can continue to lead my conventional life. I don't identify at all with professional full-time prostitutes. I would never do that, no matter how desperate I got, even if the only other choice was to go on welfare. I'm not a prostitute; I'm a normal woman who earns extra money turning tricks.

And the money, of course, is the main reason I do this. I average about fifteen hundred dollars a month in extra cash, and it's all mine—no taxes, no deductions for Social Security, disability, insurance, nothing. I make eighteen thousand a year as a secretary, which is considered very good, but it's only that high because good secretaries are hard to find and because I've been with the same company for nine years, ever since I graduated from high school But a lot of that goes for taxes and Social Security, and my take-home is only about $225 a week. You can't live on that in New York City —you can exist, but you can't live. The extra money I make turning tricks means I can have my own apartment, and that's precious to me because I hate living with roommates. My place is six hundred dollars a month, but it's a good studio in a good building on the East Side. I was brought up in the Bronx, and I've had more than my fill of that lower-middle-class life.

I try to save a hundred dollars a week, and the rest goes for clothes—a lot! I don't even try to keep track, because I love to dress well—and my other big extravagance, cabs. Cabs to work, cabs to go see customers, cabs home. The subway is terrible and reminds me of the Bronx, and buses are okay but they're just too slow.

And I spend a little more than I should on eating out all the time, because I just don't like to cook at home for myself. But this is usually just for dinner, and I stick to coffee shops and delis or the good inexpensive restaurants, so it's not really that much. On my lunch hour I'd rather go shopping or run errands and get a yogurt or something on the way back to eat at my desk.

But the money isn't the only reason I'm a part-time call girl. My second job makes my life more interesting and gives me more variety—in sex, in the people I meet, and in the places I go and the new places and new experiences that some regular customers introduce me to—great restaurants and shows and a few less-respectable things that I'll talk about later on. I like a lot of sex and a lot of variety in sex anyway, so I figure I may as well get paid for it sometimes. And the other reason is one that I guess some women today might have a hard time understanding—I really like men. I mean, I like men in the same way that some people like music or baseball or ballet. I like male company, I like the way I'm sharper and more *on* with men than with women—that kind of electricity in the air between me and him that's always there even if we're just talking about the weather. And I like their bodies—their chests and their muscles and their hardness. And of course their cocks.

And they like my body. I'm no raving beauty, but I'm attractive. I'm twenty-eight, but I look like I'm still in my early twenties. I've got good legs and a very nice ass. My tits are small but nicely shaped and with good nipples and great —what's the word—uplift. My mother is Irish and my father Italian, and I've got just the right mix of that kind of Irish clean porcelain fair look and the Italian dark hair and exotic Latin sultry thing. Cute is the word, I guess; at least, that's what my parents say—"Barbara is *cute.*"

My parents would *kill* me if they ever found out what I'm doing. They're both walking definitions of conventional, strict Catholics. But I love them, and we've always gotten along pretty well. I had a happy childhood, and I still like to go back home for the big family get-togethers on Thanksgiving and Christmas. They'd like me to call and visit more often, but they understand that I'm trying to lead my own life in the city. They wonder why I haven't gotten married yet, but I just tell them the truth—not the whole truth, but still the truth—I want to get married eventually, but I'm just not ready for it yet.

And it's kind of hard to be married when you're going to some guy's apartment four or five nights a week to do whatever he wants in bed. I never work out of my own apartment. Once in a great while, if it's a steady customer I know really well and for some reason he can't use his place that night, I'll go to a hotel, but I don't like to do that because there's always the chance that someone I know might see us. I could tell them it was just a friend, but then they'd wonder why I didn't use my own apartment. I never, ever let a customer come to my apartment or even know where I live.

I've got an unlisted telephone number, and none of my customers know my last name or where I work. They sometimes set up a date through a girl friend of mine who's also a part-timer, but I really prefer to call them when I want to work and ask them if they want to see me that night. Usually they'll say yes, or we'll set up something for the next night or another time.

I get from $50 to $150, depending on what we do: $50 is for straight sex or just a blow job, and $75 for half and half, a blow job and then a fuck. It's $100 for a tongue bath—licking and sucking the guy all over his body—and $150 if I get fucked in the ass. The $150 includes whatever else the guy wants, including a tongue bath, and the $100 includes a fuck if he wants it, but a lot of my customers who get a tongue bath like to end up with my sucking their cock until they come. If the guy wants to come twice, that's an extra $35, no matter what we did the first time. But I don't do any all-night sessions—never. That's an absolute rule.

I do four or five tricks a week because that's as much as I want to work; I want to limit this to a small part of my life. I could turn fifty tricks a week if I wanted to—and if I could handle it physically! The demand is practically unlimited, and not just because all my guys recommend me highly to their friends. It's also because we part-timers are far and away the first choice of a lot of guys looking for good sex that will cost them only money, not emotional involvement or a lot of time. This is because we're real women rather than prostitutes; we don't have that hardness and contempt for men; we're willing to do more things—including little things like taking all our clothes off—and not rush, and we enjoy what we're doing most of the time. Part of this is because we can pick and choose our customers. I only go with men I really like; if a new guy is someone who doesn't appeal to me, I simply don't see him again.

All my customers come through referrals. I never pick up men in a bar or on the street—or anywhere. There's just too much risk that way, not only of getting arrested but of getting some weirdo or dangerous nut. And I'm very careful never to deal with anyone who might ever have any contact with the company I work for.

Almost all of my steadies are high-class guys. One, I'll call him Tony, is a lawyer and, like most of my customers, is married. Another, Arnie, is a newspaper editor who's separated and lives like a single guy; he likes to take me out for dinner and shows and all that and treat me like a regular girl friend. But there's also Jerry, who's a taxi driver. He's twenty-seven, younger than most of them, and he knows New York inside out, every bar, every club, every all-night restaurant. He's a very sweet guy, and he takes me to a lot of wild places. He's also what I like to call a freelance pharmacist, but that's a whole other story that I'll get into later.

Hiding all the money is a bit of a problem; I'm always afraid that if I dumped a lot of it in the bank the tax guys would audit me someday and get suspicious and say, "How can you live like this and save all that money on eighteen grand a year?" Naturally I'd tell them that since I've got guys taking me out all the time and buying me clothes, my only real expense is the apartment, but I'm still paranoid about anything like this that could make someone suspicious. So the main way I handle all the cash—aside from spending a lot, of course!—is to stash it in lock boxes hidden away in the apartment.

But except for seeing customers, my daily routine is pretty much like everyone else's, and very regular. I go out with my boyfriend on my free nights, usually on the weekends, and I almost never stay up past midnight except on Friday and Saturday. When I do stay out till two or three during the week, it's just too hard to get up in the morning and I drag ass all day and ruin the next evening because I fall into bed by nine o'clock.

Boyfriends can be a bit of a problem when you're a part-time call girl. I've had five pretty steady lovers since I started doing this three years ago, and I've ended up telling three of them what I do part-time. Whether or not I tell just depends on what kind of guys they are and how our relationship goes along. The men I told were secure and very open-minded and willing to let me be myself, and when the time felt right, I'd bring it up in a roundabout way to see how they'd react.

I'd say, "You know, one of my girl friends has a regular job but she's a call girl part time"—which is true. If the guy seemed intrigued by the idea, we'd talk about it for a little while, and sometime later I'd say the girl friend had asked me to give it a try and would he mind if I did it. One of the two boyfriends who I didn't tell was appalled at the idea of me turning a trick and said he wouldn't be able to stand it, so I said I had just been kidding around and that was the end of it. The other guy I didn't tell got so shocked when I told him about the girl friend that I never went any further.

One reason I like to let my lovers know what's going on is that it makes my life a lot simpler. The secrecy and having to be careful all the time is the worst part of being a part-time call girl, and sometimes it can get to be a tremendous strain. I've had a couple of very close calls when the guys I didn't tell almost found out what I was doing, and I can't stand that kind of nerve-racking crisis.

Another reason is that telling makes the relationships much better. When you're constantly hiding something from your lovers, you don't feel as close to them as you should, and you can't be as open with them. This is especially important in sex. Being a part-timer made me a lot freer sexually and much more willing to ask for what I wanted and to do wild things, and of course I thought my men would love this —but not all of them did. The two guys I didn't tell seemed to be threatened by my being sexually demanding and kind of kinky. I never really understood why, but I guess they were afraid they couldn't keep up with me, or they felt it threatened their role as the dominant male, or something. But in any case this required a lot of adjustment from both of us and made the whole relationship kind of dicey. And it made me uncomfortable.

But the other three boyfriends not only said they didn't mind but got kind of excited by the idea. So after my "first" customer I made sure they were still comfortable with the idea, and then I told them I'd "started" to do it on a regular basis—the truth if not the whole truth, just a little white lie about the time scale.

One guy, Steven, was in bed with me when I told him about the girl friend's proposition, and we had made love twice, which was usually his limit. But when we started talking about my meeting my first customer and all the things I would do for him, Steven got hard as a rock again. I went down on him and sucked him off very slowly and all the while he was telling me all the things he wanted me to do to the customer—suck his nipples and his ass and his balls and let him fuck me in the ass. Steven got himself so hot that he shot his third load of the night in my mouth after what seemed like just a few seconds of my sucking him. And this is what happens with the guys I tell; they don't just tolerate it, they like it because it excites them. They get tremendously turned on when I tell them about my sexual adventures, and they want to hear every juicy detail. And in between times they're stimulated just by the idea that I'm having sex with other guys.

II. Getting Started

What I've told my boyfriends about how I got started in the business is based on the truth. I never planned to go into this. But when I was twenty-five I was having dinner with one of my best friends, Kathy, and we got into a very heavy discussion, telling each other all our problems and hangups.

We were in a restaurant in Little Italy, and as we were starting our second espressos, Kathy looked at me very seriously and said, "I'm going to tell you something about me that almost nobody knows, because I know I can trust you to keep it a secret."

"You're going to have an abortion."

"No!" Kathy laughed and I could see her get a little less tense. "You know I know better than that! I'm too careful to let things get that far. But it's—in a way you may think it's worse."

"You're on speed or smack."

"No—not *that* bad."

"Okay, no more guesses. Tell me." I could see her starting to get tense again.

"I'm a hooker."

I laughed; I really thought she was putting me on. "And all this time I believed you when you told me you go to the office every day! Can I borrow a thou?"

Kathy shook her head. "I'm *serious*, Barbara. I do it part time. I see guys five or six times a week." She looked at me, watching it sink in, and said, "You're shocked—I can tell."

"Well, yeah, sure. But why? And how? You want to tell me about it?"

Kathy could tell that I was intrigued. She looked so good sitting there across from me and so pretty, glowing with health and full of life. She's got reddish-brown hair and a *great* figure, and her skin always has a nice kind of flush that gets brighter when she's had a lot of wine or food.

She nodded. "I do want to tell you. It's something I've kept secret as long as I could—from everyone." She hesitated. "But when it's someone really close to you, like you, after a while it bothers you that you keep this hidden, and you just don't feel right. You want to tell people you trust, and you don't want to keep things from your closest friends."

Kathy lit a Vantage and ordered a brandy and started to tell me her story. "I started about a year ago. I was still going with Gary, you remember him, he's kind of a freak, and he'd been after me to do a threesome with this friend of his, Peter. I liked Peter, and I was curious enough about what it would be like to kind of toy with the idea, but I really didn't want to do it and I kept putting Gary off— without saying flatly, no, never.

"Then one night the three of us went out to dinner together and drank a lot of wine and had a great time—good talk and laughs and very relaxed, not even any mention of sex. We went back to Gary's place and smoked some grass and it just kind of happened, naturally, spontaneously. Gary had some mellow music on and I was dancing with both of them and I could feel that they both had tremendous hard-ons. Peter was stroking my ass and feeling me up while we were dancing, and I danced closer to him and started grinding myself into his hard-on. Peter unbuttoned my blouse and Gary came up behind me and undid my bra and they both started sucking my breasts—one on each. Then we moved over to the couch and took off the rest of my clothes and

Peter went down and started sucking my pussy while Gary—"

"Kathy! Save the juicy details for later, okay?" I didn't tell her I was getting turned on just hearing about it. "I can't wait to hear how the hooking started. Peter didn't start paying you, did he?"

"No, we got to be too close after that night. I screwed them both and we had a few more threesomes after that and did everything and it was great—I had some of the best times I've ever had in my life.

"Then Peter called me one day and wanted me to go to an orgy. I told him I didn't want to, that I wasn't ready for that yet. He said, 'That's the way you felt about the threesome, but once you did it you loved it.' I told him, 'That's right, but the big difference is that I *knew* you. I don't want to get into a big scene with a lot of people I don't know.' So then he played his trump card and asked if I would do it if he could get Gary to come along. I told him I'd probably feel a lot more comfortable that way and if he could persuade Gary to come, I'd go along.

"Of course, talking Gary into going was about as difficult as boiling water, so a few nights later there I was. I met a really nice guy there and went with him and did everything for him, and he was so turned on he told me he just had to see me again. I really wanted to but I thought if I started seeing him that would mean three men at once and that would be more than I could handle. So I hemmed and hawed. Then he offered me fifty bucks to see him and I thought, *What the hell. I've gone this far, threesomes and orgies, why not do it?* So I said yes. I saw him a few times and then he told me about a friend of his who wanted to see me, and this friend had a friend, and, well, here we are."

Kathy looked at me, and I could tell she was waiting for me to say something but I really didn't know what she expected me to say, so I just sat there. She laughed and said, "Are you *too* shocked?"

"No," I said. "Not really. But doesn't it—I mean, doesn't it bother that you're doing this?"

"No, it really doesn't. It did a little bit at the beginning, but that wore off quickly. Because I keep it under control. For me, it's just like having a second job working evenings at Macy's or something like that—but this is much more fun. And I set the hours. And the money! The money would make it worthwhile even if I didn't like it."

I asked Kathy how much she charged, and what her routine was, and about all the details of her double life. We must have sat in the restaurant for another hour talking about it. I was totally fascinated, but it never crossed my mind that I might do the same thing someday. It's like talking to a doctor or a lawyer about what they do; you find it terrifically interesting but you never think of going into it yourself.

At that time I was living in kind of a dumpy apartment on Amsterdam Avenue in the Eighties. I could have had a much better place if I lived with a roommate, but by then I'd discovered the hard way that I hated living with a roommate. And the television was a good companion when I wasn't going out. One night, about three or four weeks after our big heart-to-heart conversation in the restaurant, Kathy called me at home. We chatted for a while and then she said, "You remember that secret I told you about? Well, uh, one of my customers wants a little variety and would like to make it with someone new, and I was wondering if you'd like to try it."

"Kathy! Me! Are you kidding?"

"No. I thought you might like to give it a whirl—just once. If you don't like it, that's the end of it. I just thought of that old Barbara bit: 'I'll try anything once.' "

I laughed. "Yeah. Usually. But this is different. I'm kind of intrigued by the idea—it sounds kind of exciting. But I guess I'm scared, you know? Can you give me a few days to think about it?"

"Sure. Take your time—there's no rush. I know you're probably a little afraid; I certainly was the first time. But you know I wouldn't fix you up with anyone except a really good guy. I've known this man for almost a year, and he's a hundred percent okay."

"Yeah, but what does he like? . . . Anything too far out?"

Kathy laughed. "I don't know what you mean by far out, but he's not going to want to tie you up or beat you. He likes to fuck, and he loves a blow job, and he likes to take his time. He loves to have his nipples played with—that's about as kinky as he gets. But don't worry. I think you'll enjoy it."

"How much should I ask for—or have you already arranged all that?"

"Well, no, not yet, but since it's basically straight stuff and you're, you know, a 'beginner' in this, I think we'd probably set it up for fifty dollars."

"What are you going to tell him about me?"

"I just told him what you look like and that you're a good person and fun to be with and I thought he'd like you. His name is Paul, he's a lawyer, and he's a really nice guy."

"How did you meet him?"

"Through another customer. That's always how it happens. It all started with this guy I met at the orgy—he introduced me to other guys and so on. My whole business grew from this one first—seed." Kathy giggled.

All of a sudden I had a moment of disgust about the whole thing. Here was this girl I'd known for years and felt really close to and she was fucking around as a whore and now she wanted to drag me into it.

"Kathy—did you tell me about this a few weeks ago just because you wanted to recruit me?"

"No! I told you, I felt I had to confide in someone about it. And I don't manipulate my friends like that! First of all, Barbara, I don't want to 'recruit' you—there's really nothing in it for me. I'm doing it for you, because I think you might enjoy it and you can make a lot of extra money. And if you try it once and you hate it, that's the end of it. I'm certainly not going to press you to do it again."

"Yeah. I'm sorry—I shouldn't have said that. But I'm really very curious about what this would be like, and I guess I'm angry at myself for being curious and I took it out on you."

"I understand, Barbara. But like I said, you don't have to decide right this minute. Take a few days and think about it and let me know."

We said good-bye and I put the phone down and thought, *No, I don't really want to do this. I'll call Kathy next week and tell her no and then we'll just forget it.* I turned on the television, but I found I couldn't pay attention to what was on the screen. My mind kept wandering back to thinking what it would be like to go to bed with this guy I'd never seen before. I'd been with a lot of men by that time, but I'd never slept with anyone I didn't know pretty well or anyone I didn't really like. And of course I'd never been paid.

But the money didn't really matter to me as I thought about it; what intrigued me was the idea of going to bed with a total stranger and doing whatever he wanted—and I guess whatever I wanted too. I'd probably never see him again; there'd be no phone calls the next day, no involvement. It would be all—free, it would be—what did that writer call it, a flying fuck? I kept getting more and more curious about what it would be like, and when I tried to go to sleep that night I realized that there was only one way I could satisfy my curiosity.

I called Kathy the next day.

"Hi, it's Barbara. How ya doin'? Listen, if this guy is *fat,* I'm not going to do it."

Kathy laughed. "No—he's thirty-four years old, he's slim, and he's got a very good body. And I told you, he's a nice guy. You're going to be perfectly okay. And if you decide at the last minute to back out he's not going to attack you. The worst he would do is give you his card in case you ever need a lawyer!"

"Okay. Well, I want to try it. If you can set it up for Wednesday or Thursday—and early, around seven o'clock. I don't want to turn into something at midnight. And this is at his place, right? I don't want him coming over here, and I don't want to go to a hotel."

"Of course—it's always at his place. I'll call you back as soon as I set it up. You've got a date!"

It turned out to be Thursday at seven, and when I got up Thursday morning and got ready to go to the office I looked in the closet and thought, *What?* It was a work day, and I didn't want to look all seductive, but somehow I wanted to wear something special and attractive. No pants, and no innocuous tops. And it had to be something easy to get out of. I always keep these practical considerations in mind; it's my good upbringing. I finally settled on a navy blue suit and a powder blue blouse with red stripes, and heels. No nylons, which I never wear, and no bra, which I seldom wear unless it's necessary for decency with certain tops. I looked at myself in the mirror and giggled. I looked like Miss Young Executive, or Miss Secretary ready for a blind date with a doctor. A little too dressy, maybe, but nice. I took the slip of paper where I had written the address Kathy gave me, put it in my purse, and I was off.

It was hard to concentrate at work, and the time dragged, but five o'clock finally came. When I walked out of the building, I was already starting to get nervous. I felt I needed something several cuts above my usual weekday dinner so I went to the Brasserie, sat at the counter, and had onion soup and a steak—with a half-bottle of red wine. I usually just have a glass of wine or a beer, but I still felt nervous and I thought that if ever there was a night for a half-bottle, this was it. I love espresso and I usually have a double or two, but I was already so wired I decided to have just a demitasse. I sat there smoking and not wanting to look at my watch, but I did and it was six twenty. Time to go.

The address was in the Village, and I walked over to Lexington Avenue to get a cab. But I stood there for a few minutes just watching them go by. I was scared. I thought, *Do you really want to go through with this? Turn around and walk over to Park and get a cab uptown and go home.* But I said to myself, *You can't stand Paul up, and you can't run out on Kathy after all this and have Paul mad at you and mad at Kathy and Kathy angry at you. And if you don't do it, you'll spend the rest of your life wondering what it would have been like.* I stepped out into the street and put up my arm and got a cab. But on the way down, I kept thinking about the old saying that curiosity killed the cat.

The building was one of those old Village tenements on the western edge—not at all bad, but not what I'd expected as the home of a rich lawyer. I got out and rang the bell for 2C. I was running on adrenaline now, and the nervousness had gone. The door was buzzed open and I walked up the stairs.

I rang the doorbell and a handsome man opened the door and smiled at me. "Barbara? Come in."

I smiled back and walked in. He was wearing a bright red bathrobe, and boy, was he good-looking! Black hair, wet and uncombed, about six feet tall, with a rugged, muscular body. He looked fresh, as if he'd just stepped out of the shower, and youthful.

"Let me hang up your jacket and get you a drink. What would you like?"

I turned a bit so he could help me off with my suit jacket and said, "Could I have a *small* cognac?"

He gave me that warm, real smile again and motioned toward the couch. "Of course. Make yourself comfortable."

Paul went into the kitchen, and I sat down on the couch and glanced around the apartment. It was a small one-bedroom, kind of sparsely furnished, and it was comfortable enough but just didn't seem like a lawyer's home—more like a clerk's apartment. The little table in front of the couch was solid enough but looked like something I remembered from the Bronx. And the liquor was kept in a kitchen cupboard instead of at a bar or sideboard. I had a sense that something was wrong.

But even so, I felt very at ease with Paul. He was warm and relaxed and sweet, like a blind date who turns out to be wonderful. But this was even better, because I knew what was going to happen and I could relax.

Paul came back with two snifters, handed me one, and sat down on a chair across from me. I took a sip and said, "Mmm! It's Delamain. My favorite!"

"Mine too. We have so much in common! Now, are you wondering about the apartment—why it's not bigger and more luxurious?"

I laughed—mostly out of relief and surprise but also because I liked him more moment by moment. He not only had a sense of humor but gave off the right vibrations and was on the same wavelength as me.

"I was, as a matter of fact," I said. "Kathy told me you're a lawyer and quite successful, and I guess I was expecting a real liquor cabinet and all that and maybe even a maid—a French maid saying, *'Oui, oui, monsieur.'*"

Paul laughed. He had a wonderful kind of deep sexy laugh. "That's Fifi. She's in the bedroom. No, this is a second home. The main home is in Greenwich."

"Ah, I see. And at the main home are the wife and children."

"Uh-huh. Two boys and a girl."

"This apartment is just for—for assignations?"

Paul laughed again and looked at me appreciatively. *"Wonderful* word. It *is* for assignations, but it's not just that. It's not quite as bad as it sounds. There are nights when I have to work very late and can't do the commute and have to stay in the city, so that's basically what it's for."

"Very nice. You know I'd like—I mean, I guess I really shouldn't ask this—but I feel so at ease with you—"

"Go ahead. Ask anything you want."

"You're married, so why do you do this? I mean, sure you want a little variety once in a while, but you're a good-looking guy, you could get just about anyone you wanted. Why do you—do this?"

"A very good question. An interesting question. Partly it's variety without any problems. If I had a mistress or a girl friend, I'd have phone calls and entanglements and emotional involvement and problems. And I would never go to a professional prostitute because that's just not my thing. I like Kathy and enjoy her company and I have a great time with her, and it's perfect."

I smiled at him. Somehow he made me feel sexy and womanly. I said, "I'll try to be perfect," and raised my glass and made a little tap in the air with it and said, "Cheers," and we both finished our cognac. Then Paul slid out of his bathrobe and left it on the chair and came over to me and held out his hand. He had a gigantic hard-on. I took his hand with my left hand and let him pull me gently up and I put my right hand around his cock—the lady and the whore in one easy motion. He kissed me, very gently at first, then we opened our mouths and tongue-fucked, that's the only way I can describe it, hard, while I caressed his cock and balls. Then he pulled back and said, "Let's go in the bedroom." I stroked his chest—God, was he nice—and smiled at him coquettishly and said, "To see Fifi?"

Paul loved it. He laughed uproariously. "You can do her too—she loves it."

A big double bed with clean white sheets. Lamps on nightstands on each side with just the right glow. We sat down on the bed and Paul unbuttoned my blouse. "Ummm. No bra. I like that." He leaned over and ran his tongue around one nipple and stroked the other one with a finger. He was so *gentle*. I undid the skirt and slid out of that and lay back on the bed. Paul sucked first one nipple, then the other, then ran his tongue down my stomach and into my belly button. I lifted my ass off the bed so he could take my panties off, and spread my legs. I thought for a second that he was going to climb on top of me but he moved his head down and started licking my clit, back and forth, then sucking it, then sucking it and running his tongue around it at the same time. God, did he know what he was doing! I lay there moaning, and he started alternating between my clit and my cunt, rolling his tongue around my cunt and then licking my clit and driving me out of my mind. He kept at it until I started coming, and then he just did it faster and wouldn't stop when I first tried to push his head away. Finally he slowed down and came up and kissed me; I was amazed at how good I tasted!

"Your turn!" I said, and started sucking his nipples. I went down on him and started licking his balls and then his cock until he couldn't stand it any longer and he said, "Okay." I raised my head and smiled at him and he gave me that thousand-watt grin and said, "Have a seat. I feel lazy." I sat on his cock and eased it inside me slowly and then reached forward and started flicking his nipples with my fingernails. "Ummm. How did you know I like that?"

I laughed. "Oh, a little birdie told me," I said, and started moving with him and caressing his nipples. We did it slow and easy until Paul said, "Faster," and after a few moments of frantic action he came beautifully for what seemed like a whole minute. I kept on moving slowly to give him the last bits of pleasure and then lay down beside him and gave him a sweet, lingering kiss.

"You're wonderful," Paul said.

"You too. It was great. I was afraid it was going to be just wham, bam, thank you, ma'am."

"Oh, no, never—I like to take my time. And let's do this again sometime. Can I call you?"

I shook my head. "Uh-unh. I want to be Miss Mystery.

But I'll call you whenever you like—or you can set something up through Kathy."

Paul took out a business card from a drawer in the nightstand and wrote down a number on it. "Okay. Call me at work, or call me here—that's this number—and leave a message on the answering machine. But either way, when you call you're Mrs. Hansen, and if I'm not in when you call me at work and my secretary asks what it's about, just tell her it's a personal call. And if she asks for your number, just tell her I already have it."

"You don't have to worry. I know all about secretaries, and I'm always very discreet. I'll give you a call at work—next Tuesday or Wednesday?"

"Monday or Tuesday is best. Then we can set something up either for that night or sometime during the week. It'll never be Friday or on the weekend. And it'll always be here. But, Barbara, whatever you do, never, ever call me at home."

"Oh, you don't have to tell me that. Like I said, I'm very discreet, and the more secrecy there is the better I like it."

Paul smiled at me. "We're on the same wavelength, aren't we. Now, are you going to be all right getting home?"

"Oh, sure, I'll get a cab. That's my great weakness, taxis, even though I can't really afford them. But I get my fill of the train going back and forth to work."

"Since you're not driving, how about a nightcap?"

I laughed. "Paul, you're trying to lead me down the path of ruination. I had more wine than I should have had at dinner, and I had that cognac, and now—but you know I can't resist Delamain, don't you? You're getting to know all my weaknesses. Just a *little* bit, okay? Just three sips' worth."

Paul gave me a pat on the ass and went to get the cognac. I got dressed—where were those shoes? Oh, under the couch —and wondered what I was supposed to do about the money. I didn't feel like asking for it right out, but what was

I supposed to say? "Didn't you forget something?" "Fork it over, buster." "Gee, I don't have any cab fare." I went back to the couch feeling a bit uncomfortable about the whole thing and cursing myself for not having had the brains to ask Kathy about how this was handled.

Paul was back in the chair across from the couch; the cognac was on the table, and next to it was a white envelope. I picked up the envelope and put it in my bag and said, "Thank you," feeling very relieved but still a little bit strange. My first paid performance—another kind of virginity gone.

Paul lifted his glass to me and said, "Cheers. And you're welcome."

I laughed. He was kidding my formal politeness. I raised my glass and said, "Cheers," and downed the cognac. It was very little, really just about three sips, and I finished it in one voluptuous swallow and said, "Where's the rest, you stingy bastard? There isn't enough here to intoxicate a fly."

Paul smiled. "Barbara, you're insatiable. Promise me you'll go straight home and go to sleep without getting into any more mischief."

"I promise. And I'll call you next week."

I got up and we kissed goodnight and Paul took me to the door and kissed me again and said, "Sweet dreams."

I went down the stairs and walked to the corner and got a cab right away. I felt great—glowing and happy. I opened the envelope in the cab and found five crisp new tens. I thought, *This is more than a whole day's pay after deductions.* And I was amazed at how much I had liked it. I had thought it was going to be kind of an ordeal, but it had turned out to be just the opposite—I had enjoyed it tremendously.

It was because Paul had been so warm and gentle and wonderful. I knew I wanted to see him again, but as I took the money out of the envelope and put it in my purse, I thought, *Where is this going to lead you, Barbara, old girl? Are you going to turn into a call girl at the age of twenty-five?* I had a sudden vision of quitting my job and getting a big co-op on Park Avenue with pink satin sheets and blue lights in the bedroom and my parents coming over to visit and my mother asking, "What is it, Barbara? Did you win in the lottery?" and me yawning and stretching in my brief black negligee and saying, "Ah, no, Mother. I just got myself a sugar daddy."

No! I wanted to keep my straight life—but I wanted this other thing too. If Kathy could have them both and keep them separate, maybe I could too. But I had liked this session with Paul *too* much. It was possible to get hooked on this and OD on it just as I often had with espresso and cigarettes. Only this was much worse and much more complicated. The cab had reached midtown; we were going up Sixth Avenue, and I stared out the window at the New York evening and at the people out for a night on the town and thought about my future. By the time I got home, I had decided to call Kathy and ask her advice.

I got home and undressed and looked through my mail and thought about what I would ask Kathy. Then the phone rang, and it was her.

"Hello, Barbara, you *sinful* bitch. How was it?"

I laughed. "You couldn't wait to hear about it, could you? I was just going to call you. It was wonderful. He's such a hunk. And he was so considerate and gentle and nice."

"I told you he was a sweet guy. And I told him it was your first time, so he was probably even gentler than usual. I wouldn't even be surprised if he let you sit on top and run the show."

"Kathy! You do get personal, don't you? But why didn't you tell me he was married?"

"Oh, I thought you might not like it or might get the wrong idea or get your middle-class morals all in a dither about tricking with a married man."

"No—no, in a way that somehow made it seem better or less threatening. More intimate and more exciting, somehow. I don't know exactly why."

"Barbara, you're terrible. You're just like me—you have no scruples. Are you going to see him again?"

"I'd really like to, but—but, well, I don't really know how deeply I want to get into this."

"That's entirely up to you, you know. You just do it as much as you feel like. You're in control of everything. It's not like a part-time job where you have to show up all the time or have to produce a certain amount of work to keep the job. You do it when and with who you want to, that's all."

"But you know me, Kathy. When I like something, I tend to overdo it. And I like my life now—I don't want to screw it up."

"You can't screw it up as long as you're very careful. You never give anyone your last name or your phone number or let them know where you live or work. And you never, never, see anyone who isn't known and recommended. But you do have to keep it down to just a few times a week. The danger is that if you get too greedy, it starts to interfere with your regular life just because you don't have enough *time* to take care of everything. But why don't you just see Paul for now and see how it goes, and if you want then I can fix you up with one or two other guys?"

"I guess that's the best way to handle it. Just take it as it comes and see what happens."

"Sure. You want to have dinner Saturday? Gino's or that place in Little Italy?"

"I've got a date with Michael Saturday."

"Aha! Boyfriends! They can be a problem. Don't tell him, whatever you do. And there's something else, you know? You're going to end up being a little looser and wilder in bed, and he might suspect that you've been getting into some strange stuff."

"Oh, he'd like that. And a little jealousy might do him good. But I see what you mean. Kathy, the temptation to tell him is going to be overwhelming, but I guess I'd have to be crazy to do that."

Kathy and I made plans to have dinner on Sunday, and I started worrying about the date with Michael. He and I had been seeing each other steady for about six months and had a really good thing going. We both liked jazz and Italian food and we got along great most of the time. He was a real estate broker I met one night at Maxwell's Plum; he made good money and was very generous and warm. Michael wasn't the greatest lover I'd ever had, but he was more than adequate in bed, and overall I liked him a lot. He just wasn't *exciting* in the same way that Paul had been. The money had absolutely nothing to do with that. It's just that, although I felt a great deal of affection for Michael and the sex with him was basically satisfying, he didn't turn me on all the way or even nearly so—maybe about seventy percent. All right, make that sixty-nine percent.

A date with Michael had the same virtues and faults as Michael himself, I guess. It was dinner, and then a jazz club or a movie, or once in a while a play, and then home to bed, usually at his place. Once in a while we'd double-date with Kathy or someone else or go to a party, but otherwise it was the same routine—very pleasant and enjoyable but not exactly wildly exciting or different or new. No sense of adventure or thrill of discovery, I guess is what I'm trying to say.

But our date that Saturday was different—because I felt different. We had lasagna and sausage at Forlini's and went to the Vanguard to hear Jim Hall, and all the time I found myself wickedly tempted to say, "Oh, you know what I did Thursday night?" And Michael would think I was going to tell him about a new restaurant or a movie or an evening of drinking with Kathy, and I would say, "I made fifty dollars fucking," and the poor thing would choke on his lasagna or scream right in the middle of one of Jim Hall's most soulful guitar solos. Of course I didn't. But I felt funny being with him that night. I hadn't made love with anyone but Michael for the last six months, and now all of a sudden I had cheated—in spades. Would it show on me in some subtle way? Could he tell? Would he pick something up from the slight discomfort I felt? I finally decided, *No, not to worry,* because Michael was not all that sensitive.

But when we left the Vanguard and got into a cab to go back to his place I started to feel a little antsy. I felt extra horny and wanted to be able to let myself go the same way I had with Paul. Do something new, at least. If Michael suspected anything, I'd just tell him the truth: that I was feeling wicked tonight and thought we could start having a little variety in bed. Not the whole truth, but the truth.

The usual routine was almost always the same. We'd undress—by ourselves; we hadn't undressed each other in a long time—and there'd be a bit of kissing and tit caressing and a little sixty-nine and then we'd fuck, usually with him on top. But this time when he started stroking my breasts I leaned over and flicked my tongue back and forth over his nipple, then started licking and sucking it. Michael gave a little moan and took his hand away from my breast and settled back on the bed. I felt a little twinge of excitement— if he was willing to be the passive one tonight, then our moods matched perfectly. I started sucking really hard on first one nipple then the other and stroking his cock and balls with my hand. Then I turned around and we did our sixty-nine for a while, but when we stopped I didn't lie down as usual but swung around and sat on top of him and put his cock inside me. Michael gave me a great big grin of surprise and pleasure and started to move with me, and I suddenly understood—he wasn't opposed to new stuff, he just didn't have the imagination or the courage or whatever to propose it himself. I was getting really hot now and I started riding him really hard and squeezing his nipples and we came together better than we had in a long time. I lingered on top of him for a few minutes like I had with Paul, then I got off slowly and lay down beside him and gave him a long tonguey kiss. He just gave me a little look and said, "Wow," and I had to laugh. "That was nice," he said.

"Oh, just a spur of the moment thing. I suddenly had an idea, and I felt like doing it this way."

"We should try new things more often," Michael said. "We were getting into a little bit of a rut, doing the same thing all the time."

I smiled at him. Dear, sweet Michael—not a single suspicious bone in his body. I said gently, "I guess maybe we both thought so, but we just felt so comfortable with the old routine—or it didn't occur to either one of us to bring up the idea of something new."

Michael looked at me seriously. "Maybe we should talk more about sex."

"Yeah, sure, but it has to be *spontaneous,* you know? You just have to feel it." Then I gave him another deep kiss and said, "But, baby, I'm open to suggestions."

Michael was hard again, so we did a long scrumptious sixty-nine and finished that way, for old times' sake, I guess, and went to sleep.

The next night at dinner with Kathy, I told her all about the night with Paul and then told her what had developed with Michael. She let me talk and pour it all out and listened understandingly. I realized that she was the closest and most loyal friend I'd ever had.

I told Kathy that I was going to call Paul tomorrow and asked her if that was all right with her.

"Barbara, come on. You don't have to get permission from me. You don't even have to check in with me or let me know; this is your business. We're not in competition, and I've got five times as many opportunities as I want to handle. Just do whatever you feel like, but if you ever need help or advice about this from me, call."

The next morning I could hardly wait to call Paul. "Mrs. Hansen" got right through with no trouble, and we set it up for seven o'clock Tuesday night. Same time, same place. Even though this was only the second time, it was already taking on the feeling of a comfortable routine.

But there was little routine about the way Paul liked to have sex. Like last time, he had just taken a shower, but tonight there was no bathrobe and he was naked when he opened the door to let me in. I tossed my bag onto the couch and gave him a very deep kiss and stroked that beautiful big hard cock. When we came up for air, he said, "Cognac tonight, Mrs. Hansen?" and I said, "Later. Right now I just want Mr. Hansen."

We went into the bedroom and Paul took my clothes off, with kisses and licks along the way—breasts when the blouse came off, behind the knees after he took the skirt off, and pussy after the panties. He gave such wonderful head, but this time after I came he didn't resist when I moved away but just said huskily, "Turn over." I said, "Oh, *yeah,*" and turned over, maybe a little too quickly—too anxious! A few guys had done this to me before, and I loved it beyond words, but I'd never been able to bring myself to ask for it. Paul teased me for a minute by just licking the cheeks of my ass, then circling in closer and closer. Finally he put his tongue in and licked gently and slowly. I moaned and arched up and tried to spread myself open wider. Paul rimmed me for a few fantastic minutes and then lay back on the bed and said, "My turn!"

At that point I would have done just about anything for him. I gave him a super tongue bath, practically from head to toe, licking his ears and neck and armpits and nipples and tonguing his belly button and sucking his balls. I sucked his cock for a minute or so and then told him to turn over. I'd only done this before for one other guy, a former boyfriend I'd been crazy about. Paul turned me on the same way but even more, and he was so clean. I rimmed him for a few minutes and he went wild, but finally he pulled away and told me to lie down, and we had a good old-fashioned fuck with him on top. Paul had gotten so hot by then that I was afraid he was going to come too soon, but he had great control and lasted a long time, and I came again. Paul gave me a tender kiss to wrap it all up and rolled off.

"You know, Barbara, you're not too bad."

"You're kind of all right yourself. You know, sometimes I think I envy your wife."

"Well, don't. It's not the same. It's a different kind of situation."

I could tell by Paul's tone that I had said the wrong thing. He obviously didn't want to elaborate on what he had just said, but I thought I could sense what he meant anyway. His wife probably wouldn't do certain things, or he wouldn't even ask her to do them, and in any event it was different with her—it was kind of old-shoe and less abandoned, less kinky. And it certainly wasn't free of worries about any emotional consequences. I was beginning to understand: the fact that Paul was paying me made everything in a way freer and more open and sexier. Because there was so much less at stake emotionally, there was a great sense of freedom; you felt that "everything goes" with the sex because the sex was all there was. There was no relationship to be affected, no future and no past, no subtle bartering about emotions or activities outside the bedroom. The bartering had already been taken care of, and there were no activities outside the bedroom. And there was the direct, demanding, "I want this" aspect of paying. It was like, if you borrow a coat from a friend, you take the one she gives you with gratitude, but if you go to buy one, you say, I want this kind of material and this color and this style, and I want it altered. You make your demands politely, of course, or even, as Paul did, with a kind of gracious and elegant subtlety, but they're still demands, and they still represent control. Money is power, and power is potency.

I was silent for a minute or so, thinking about this, then I reached over and caressed Paul's chest and said, "I'm sorry. It's none of my business. I was just trying to say that you're not only good in bed but you serve wonderful cognac."

Paul laughed. "Okay. I guess I can take a hint. Let's go in the living room. Or would you like it served in bed?"

"No, the living room is fine." I sensed that it was time, as Kathy liked to say, to get set to get ready to begin to go.

On the way home, I put the five ten-dollar bills in my purse one at a time. I thought again what I had on Thursday: this was more than a day's pay after deductions. And there had been a hundred dollars extra in less than a week. This money was solving problems for me. I could pay bills that had been hanging around too long and could get them off my mind.

Looking back on it now, I guess it was at that moment that I was first hooked on what would be my new life, when I realized that the extra money would bring peace of mind. But then, at that moment, I didn't realize that I was hooked; I was still telling myself that it was just going to be a matter of seeing Paul once a week or so. *Like a class that meets one evening a week or a weekly dance lesson,* I thought, and giggled to myself.

But there were two things that made me go beyond that. One was that I couldn't help focusing on the thought that if one visit a week meant an extra fifty dollars, four visits would mean an extra two hundred dollars. I would fantasize about what I could do with all that extra cash—get a better apartment in a better neighborhood, buy more clothes, eat at better restaurants. I'd start thinking about this, and I'd get carried away and figure that six times a week would mean three hundred dollars—or even more if I could charge seventy-five or a hundred for the kinky stuff. But then I'd pull myself back down to earth with the realization that six times a week would mean the whole thing was getting out of hand.

And the second thing was curiosity. Just as it had been

curiosity that got me started, it was curiosity that took me further along. I found myself wondering all the time what it would be like to do other guys. Maybe they wouldn't all be as great as Paul, but they would be different. There were new things to discover and experiences waiting that maybe I hadn't even dreamt of.

By the time the week was out, I had decided to go with the flow and ask Kathy and Paul if they could recommend another guy or two.

I was on my way.

III.   The Men

On my next date with Paul, I asked him if he could introduce me to some other guys. "Sure," he said. "How many would you like, and what kind? I can turn you on to about thirty of them—young or old, dark-haired, blond, or bald."

"I'll take 'em all! Actually, I think I'd better settle for just one or two. Pick out the two best—and not *too* kinky, please."

"Barbara, come on. I assure you I'm not intimately familiar with all the details of their sexual preferences. Let's see. The best by far is Tony—he's a lawyer too and a very nice guy and I think you two will really dig each other. He's the son of an Italian immigrant, and he's worked his way up to a lot of money, but he's very down-to-earth. And who else . . . oh, Mitchell! You'd like him, and he's a very interesting case. He's only twenty-nine, and he's always *very* horny. I suspect he doesn't get much action. Here are their numbers, but give me a chance to tell them you're going to call."

"I'll wait two days—it'll be hard to wait, because I really need some strange stuff, but I'll be patient."

"I'll show you some strange stuff, baby," Paul said, reaching over and stroking my neck, and I kissed him, and as we started off I thought of that book or song someone wrote called "Am I Getting Paid for This?" Somehow it just didn't seem right to be getting paid when you're having so much fun.

I told myself that I shouldn't expect Tony and Mitchell to

be as great as Paul. But they turned out to be just as wonderful and interesting, only in very different ways. They were both very nice guys, and with both it was, as they say, the start of a beautiful friendship.

Tony was married, so I had to call him at his office, and naturally I had to be very discreet. When his secretary asked who was calling I said, "Barbara," and she said, "Just a moment, Miss, Miss—?" She had a wonderful voice and an English accent, and she was too classy to just say, "Barbara *who?*"—which is the kind of thing I say when people call my boss and don't give their last names. It annoys me too; I call them the unknown callers. I hesitated a moment but then, thank God, the Italian word for "unknown" that I had heard my father use popped into my head and I said, "Miss Ignoto."

"If you can hold just a moment, please, Miss Ignoto, Mr. Victor will be right with you." What class, I thought, an inspiration to all us secretaries, and I kind of hoped that she didn't speak Italian.

My new name certainly didn't ring any bells with Tony, and he came on kind of formal and distant until I said, "I'm Barbara—I think Paul told you I was going to call," and then his voice blossomed into great warmth and enthusiasm. "Oh, *yes.* I'd love to meet you. How about dinner tonight at six thirty—at La Grenouille?"

"Grenouille? Great! I've never been there—but of course I've heard of it." I added that so I wouldn't sound like a complete Bronxite, but then I realized it sounded stupid after I had just said "Great!" Oh, well.

Anyway, it's one of the best French restaurants in New York, and I was looking forward to it all day. I wasn't dressed for it, but six thirty gave me just enough time to go home and change.

I got to the restaurant barely on time, and when I walked in I was completely bowled over—it was even more than I'd expected. There were beautiful fresh flowers everywhere and a wonderful glowing light that was somehow bright and soft at the same time, and just inside the door was a sideboard heaped with fantastic-looking food—salads, fresh asparagus, cold fish and paté, juicy strawberries, a floating island and pastries and big bowls of dessert sauces. I stood there a few seconds just staring at it and then turned around and the maître d'hotel, a short but sexy-looking guy, smiled at me and said, "Good evening," with a French accent and a little lift of his eyebrows.

"Good evening. Mr. Victor, please."

"Ah, yes"—a great big smile of recognition and a knowing, congratulatory look for me. "Mr. Victor." He led me to a banquette right across from a gigantic bouquet. There were more flowers on the table, and an empty place next to me on the banquette. I was glad I had arrived first, because it gave me a chance to look around and drink in the beauty of the place. A waiter came over and asked me what I would like; I would have loved a glass of white wine but I was curious to see what Tony might order—maybe champagne?—so I said, "I think I'll wait for the gentleman, thank you," and he gave me one of those super-sexy French smiles. I was already charmed out of my pants and the evening had hardly begun.

The restaurant was still less than half-full, and I was doing a bit of discreet people-watching when I saw the maître d' headed toward me with a wiry, dark-haired man, good-looking in that intense kind of Italian way. They came to the table and the maître d' pulled it out for Tony, but before he sat down he stopped and said, "Barbara. You look wonderful. How are you?"

I held out my hand and he took it for a moment and then sat down and I said, *"Grazie tante. Come va?"*

He was delighted. "Aha. You're Italian."

I laughed. "How could I not be, with a name like Ignoto?"

He grinned and said, "I won't ask about your real name. But you speak Italian beautifully."

"Actually not. I'm afraid you've just heard fifty percent of my vocabulary."

"I'll teach you a lot more. Now, do you like champagne?"

"I love it. And I love this place—I've never been to a restaurant like this before."

"Well, I'm surprised. You're so attractive that I'd imagine you being taken to a great restaurant every night."

"I would like nothing better, but I'm really just a poor girl from the Bronx. Pronounced 'Bron-nyx,' of course."

"We'll have to widen your horizons—although Paul tells me they're already delightfully wide."

I laughed. "Paul's terrific—I'm going to have to make him my agent. I just hope he didn't tell you *too* much. But I'm going to love having my horizons widened—I'm developing a taste for this level of living awfully fast."

"Speaking of taste, what would you like for dinner?"

"I'd want a bit of *everything* I saw on that cold table—except the cold asparagus. Can I get asparagus with hollandaise instead?"

"You can have anything you want. How about a selection of those cold appetizers, and chicken with tarragon and the asparagus—or a Dover sole?"

I said they both sounded marvelous, and Tony suggested he order one and I the other and we could split. The food was superb, the best I've ever had in my life, as was the wine —a Montrachet. Suddenly I understood, for the first time, what it meant to be rich. I had always thought of it in terms of having no worries and not having to think all the time about whether you could do this or afford that—you could relax and just *live*. But now I saw that it was much more than that: it was that you lived at an entirely different level. I had never eaten like this or known anyone who did, and it was not a meal you would prepare at home, even if you could get the fresh Dover sole and even if you did have two days free to shop and cook. But for Tony this was not a once-in-a-lifetime occasion; it was just dinner. He had lunch or dinner here once or twice a week, he told me, and of course I understood that if he was taking me here, who was basically just a piece of ass for him, it was no big deal. By the time we got to dessert, a Grand Marnier soufflé, I realized how much I wanted to be able to have experiences like this as just a regular part of my life.

And we had a wonderful time with each other. We talked about everything—food and friends and work—everything except sex. I liked Tony tremendously, and I could see why Paul had put him at the top of the list.

I asked for espresso, and Tony said, "No real espresso here—not what Italians like you and me are used to—but they do have very fine café filtre."

"No espresso! What a dump! I was going to ask you if you'd take me here on every date, but now I think I'll have to insist on a halfway decent restaurant."

"Barbara, let me tell you something. I mean seriously. I must admit that I hadn't planned to make this a regular part of the deal; this was mostly to get to know each other and to start things off on the right foot. But I like you a lot—you're an open, genuine person with no pretensions—and I'd love to make dinner part of the routine, if you'd like. The only problem for me is time; I have to spend some evenings with my family and I often have business meetings or work late. But as often as I can, I'd like nothing better than to take you to dinner. I want this to be like it is with Kathy and not just a strictly business deal; it works out better for everyone that way."

I smiled at him. "I'm with you. And I'll be delighted and grateful whenever you can do it." I was intensely curious about his family, but I remembered how Paul had reacted when I'd said something about his and thought it had better wait until much later—if ever. I guessed that those guys felt guilty about being with me, thought it made them not really a good husband or father, and they wanted to keep our time together walled off as a separate part of their lives. Of course, so did I, so I could understand that.

Tony's firm kept an apartment for him on Fifty-eighth Street, and since it was so close to the restaurant and the evening was so nice, we walked. I wanted to walk off the effects of all that wine and food, so I asked Tony if we could walk a few minutes more and he said, "Sure—anything you want. Within reason." I took his arm and we strolled for another fifteen minutes, checking out some of the shop windows.

The apartment was small but luxurious. I sat down on the couch and kicked off my shoes, and Tony took off his jacket and tie and asked me if I'd like a drink. "I've had too much already, but I can't resist a little cognac. And I'd love to get comfortable, if you don't mind."

"Mind? May I help?"

I gave him a sweet sexy smile. "Sure. You can do anything you want, Tony," and I stood up and wrapped my arms around him and gave him a passionate French kiss.

When we came up for air, he looked into my eyes and said, "Anything?"

I laughed. "Well, I'm not sure what you have in mind. Can we discuss the cognac first while we get me comfortable?"

Tony put his hands on the straps of my dress and slid them off my shoulders. "I have a good selection." He let the dress fall around my hips and looked hungrily at my bare breasts. Then he put one hand on each breast and caressed them. "There's Cordon Bleu, Delamain, Hine Triomphe, Hennessy Extra."

"Delamain's my favorite. Squeeze them. But tonight is my night for new experiences. A little harder. And I've never had the Hine."

Tony squeezed my breasts again and then stroked my nipples and pulled the dress down around my ankles, and I

43

stepped out of it. "Hine is the best. It's delicious—the second-best taste in the world."

Tony pulled my panties down and set me gently on the couch so he could pull them all the way off.

"Oh, really?" I said. "And what is the best taste in the world?"

"One that you may not be familiar with. Now, sit up there," he said, indicating the top of the back of the couch. I sat on the top and leaned back against the wall, and Tony sat on the couch and spread my legs and started eating me, first rolling his tongue around inside my cunt and then going up to my clit and licking it up and down and sucking it, and then going back inside. I stopped moaning long enough to say, "Oh, I get it. The best taste in the world is chicken with tarragon."

Tony started laughing and had to pull away. "No! Soufflé Grand Marnier!"

"Oh, of course." I put my foot at the top of his shirt and started rubbing his chest and said, "Would you like to get comfortable, Mr. Victor? And may I help?"

Tony got up and took my hand and said, "You may. But let's go in the bedroom."

We walked into the bedroom and I unbuttoned Tony's shirt and helped him off with it, then sucked his nipples and stroked his hard-on through his pants. We lay down on the bed and I took Tony's pants and shorts off and started sucking his balls. Then I licked his cock, slowly and teasingly, before taking it in my mouth and sucking it. "Let's do it together," he said, and I swung around and put my pussy over his face. We did a sixty-nine for a while and then Tony lifted me off and said, "Barbara, do you like Greek?"

"You mean in the ass?"

"Yeah. If you don't, that's okay."

"I've never done it that way. I'd like to try it, but just—not right now. I don't think I'm ready for that yet. But

44

anything else you want. I'd love to suck your ass and swallow your come."

Tony didn't say anything but just gave me a big smile and turned over, getting up on his knees. I licked and sucked his asshole and stroked his hard cock gently with one hand. Finally he couldn't stand it anymore and turned over on his back. I started sucking his cock, fast and hard, but he said, "No—real slow and easy," and I sucked him off very, very slowly, stopping once or twice to just lick on his cock, especially around the head. Then when I could feel him getting ready to come he said, "Okay," and I sped up a little and he came in powerful spurts and I swallowed his hot come, keeping my mouth on him a long time to make sure I got every drop. I'd only done that once or twice before, when I was especially turned on with a lover, but tonight with Tony I just felt exceptionally freaky. Almost freaky enough to do the Greek—but not quite. That could wait for next time.

Tony kissed me tenderly and murmured, "You're wonderful," then moved his head down and started licking and sucking my nipples. He did that for just the right amount of time, then moved down and started eating me again. He knew just how to do it; he'd suck my clit gently, then lick it up and down, gradually increasing the pressure. By this time Tony had a hard-on again, but he sucked me until he could sense I was getting close to coming, then climbed aboard in the old-fashioned position. He was a wonderful lover; he moved slowly and varied his thrusts, going in very deep and then almost pulling out, moving just the tip of his cock in and out. He kept this up for a long time and then started going faster and deeper and we came together in one of those floating moments that you think may last forever and that take you out of the world into your own little private mini-eternity.

We held each other for a while and then Tony kissed me lightly on the lips, very gently and tenderly, and lay back on the bed with his arm around me. We looked into each other's eyes and smiled. There was no need to say anything. I felt very warm and loving and loved.

Then, *bang,* all of a sudden it hit me what this really was, and all at once I had a terrible sense of emptiness, and the wonderful safe warm feeling faded away into sadness and a strange kind of loneliness.

Tony felt me tense and took his arm away. "What's the matter?"

I looked at him and shrugged. "You know—it's not—it's not really—" and I started crying. I couldn't even say it. I felt so terribly alone—and just moments before I had felt so close to him.

"Oh. I see. I understand." He stared up at the ceiling, looking sad and thoughtful. But, I thought, was he sad for the same reason I was, or was he just unhappy that his pleasant evening with his new playgirl had taken a messy turn and now he was going to have to deal with a sobbing female? But he did really like me; I could sense that, I thought—but maybe just because I was supposed to. And the things he had done for me in bed—he didn't have to, it was because he liked me. Or maybe just because it made things better for him. I felt I was losing my grip on reality. I couldn't sort out what was real and what was part of the deal—but I knew some of it, part of it, *was* real, and that made it worse. It would have been much simpler if there had been no dinner and I had just gone to his apartment and he had fucked me and paid me. At least then I would have understood what was going on.

I stopped crying. Tony looked at me and said softly, "I know what it is, but I don't know what to say. It's complicated, because it's not just an arrangement and it's not just a friendship. But I don't want to turn it into just an arrangement, and I hope you don't either. I'd be very unhappy if you did. And it will be a friendship—or I hope it will be. I'd be very, very unhappy if you didn't want it as a friendship. But it can't be *just* that, first of all because that wouldn't be fair to you. I'm married, and I have a family and many obligations, and I simply can't get involved in a real relationship no matter how much I'd like to. If that was all it was, it wouldn't be worth it to you—I mean, worth it to you emotionally, not just the other way. I would feel I was cheating you. This way it's at least clear where we stand. But in another way, of course, it's ambiguous—it's just one of those things in life that you have to accept as ambiguous and take for what it is."

I was silent for a moment, thinking about it, and Tony said, "I'm sorry. Do I sound too much like a lawyer?"

I laughed; I couldn't help it. "As a matter of fact, yes. But maybe the jury is still out—or maybe it isn't. I don't know; I'm too confused. I need time to think this through and sort it out." I reached out and took his hand. "But I do want to call you again. Okay?"

"Okay? Wonderful. Of course I want you to call me again."

We smiled at each other and I started to get up, and then it hit me. "Tony!"

"Yes?"

"Where the hell is my cognac?"

Tony laughed. "My God! You're right! I don't keep my promises, do I?"

"I'll forgive you this time. But I really would like to try that Hine and I think I could really use it."

I got dressed in the living room as Tony got the Hine Triomphe. He brought me the cognac, which turned out to be excellent, and an envelope. *Thank God for those envelopes,* I thought. If he had just handed me the cash, I would truly have felt like a whore, but that envelope somehow made everything seem all right; it looked so clean and white and pristine, as if it could have contained a card folded around rose petals. And we didn't have to talk about it; we hadn't discussed how much I would get, and I just assumed Paul had told Tony what the going rate was. The last thing I wanted to do now was have to bargain about it, and if Tony had said something like, "Well, I came twice, so I'll have to give you eighty dollars," that would have made me feel terrible. But Tony had too much class to say anything like that. Anyway, we finished the cognac and talked about how I should call him for the next time and where was the best place for me to catch a cab home, and I left, with a goodnight kiss and a "Sweet dreams."

Sweet dreams. Sweet man. But bittersweet young woman, thinking so hard in the cab that she barely noticed the beautiful evening and the ride across Central Park. This parttime job no longer looked as simple and easy as Kathy had made it sound and as it had seemed with Paul. Had the times with Paul just been beginner's luck, with the newness and novelty of it all masking the problems? But although I liked Paul immensely, I didn't feel as close to him as I had with Tony. But it wouldn't pay to get infatuated with these guys; they weren't about to sweep me off to their suburban houses and divorce their wives and tell their kids, "Here's Barbara, she's going to be your new mommy." And why did they do this anyway? Not just for variety, but because they could do things they probably didn't want to ask their wives to do.

Maybe this thing wasn't such a good idea after all. And was it going to take me further than I wanted to go? Was that Barbara, that nice girl who used to go to church and go to confession and be a good daughter, saying, "I'd love to suck your ass and swallow your come"? What would be the expression on dear old Father Coughlan's face if he heard that? But I didn't think those things were wrong; I thought they were wonderful. It's just that I was afraid that one thing would lead to another and I'd end up doing things that I *didn't* think were wonderful, or going with the wrong men. But I didn't have to do those things or see anyone I didn't like. And if it hadn't been for my going ahead, I never would have met those men I liked so much—or gone to Grenouille.

But I had a boyfriend—a guy I felt a great affection for. But he just wasn't as exciting as those men. Maybe Paul and Tony turned me on so much because they were strange stuff and forbidden fruit—exactly as I was exciting to them because I was strange stuff and forbidden fruit. And I had enjoyed those times with them terrifically, and I loved having the extra money. So what was wrong? *What is wrong,* I thought, *is very clear: getting my mind screwed up with all these questions, but this, but that, but but but, and getting confused and worried.* But not only that—also not knowing how to handle feeling too close to Tony or even if that was good or bad.

The only way to stop the buzzing in the brain, I finally decided, was to see a shrink or talk it over with Kathy, and Kathy was far and away the better choice. When I got home, I called her and said I needed to have a long talk with her, and we set up a dinner date for the next night. Then I realized I had been thinking so hard, I hadn't even opened the envelope. It held two fifty-dollar bills. I smiled. That much was not ambiguous or confusing. That made a lot of things all right.

Kathy and I met in our favorite place in Little Italy, the same restaurant where she had first revealed her second life to me. We had salads and scampi and I told her all about the evening with Tony and my confusion.

Kathy listened closely and when I was finished she looked at me seriously and said, "We come here a lot, right?"

"Yeah," I said, puzzled; I couldn't see what she was getting at.

"And the owner and the waiters like us a lot, right? I mean, of course they like us because we're customers, but they also really like us as people, don't they?"

"Yes, I think they do—I mean, I know they do. It's obvious and it's sincere."

"But they never feed us for free, right? Oh, once in a while they treat us to a Sambuca after dinner, but we always pay for our meal, and we never don't leave a tip. It's like, if you opened a record store, you wouldn't give your friends free records all the time, because a business is a business."

"I get the point. And it's a good one. And I understand that this other thing is a business. That's not really my problem; I can deal with that. But our business is different because it involves something that can get all tangled up with your feelings whether you want it to or not."

Kathy nodded. "I know—you're absolutely right. And I've had a problem or two that way myself. But there are two ways I've learned to handle that. One is to have a real love—or at least a real lover, a boyfriend. If you have that, then if you fall for a customer it shouldn't bother you that much. It's part of keeping this life separate from your real life. And you've got Michael."

"I know, and I like him. It's just that he seems so old-shoe compared to these guys. I know that's partly because something new and something you can't have always seems new and intriguing. But I think it's also because he really *is* dull compared to them. And in my head I know I can never have a real affair with Tony, but emotionally I still want to."

"Well, would it help if you stopped doing this?"

"Then I wouldn't see them at all. I don't want to stop this —I like it. And I need the money."

"Well, maybe you need a new boyfriend, that's all."

"But I don't want to dump Michael, and I might not ever get a guy like Tony or Paul. And I don't want to go through the searching and have to start all over from the beginning with a new guy. I guess there's a good side to that old-shoe feeling. Anyway, you said you've got two ways to deal with this. What's the other one?"

"Ah. The other one is part of my whole life philosophy: that most of the time you should just enjoy the moment for what it's worth—just enjoy it and be happy with it without thinking about it or worrying about it and trying to relate it to everything else in life. Like a good meal, like this—you can worry about whether everything you're eating and drinking is healthy and how many calories it has and whether it will hurt your appetite for the next meal or whether you should have fish tonight because you had meat last night. Or you can just order whatever you feel like having and *enjoy* it, without thinking about any of those things."

"That's good. That's so right. Kathy, you should be a shrink. No—I'm serious. I think that's some of the best advice I've ever gotten. If I can just do that, I think I'll be okay."

Kathy smiled at me warmly. "You're making me feel good. And since I'm handing out advice, maybe you should leave these guys be for a week or so and try someone else. Who was that other guy Paul recommended? The accountant?"

"Oh. Mitchell. You don't know him?"

"No—I know Tony, but not Mitchell." She laughed. "But I wouldn't be at all surprised if I get to know Mitchell soon. Call him up and let me know what happens—I'll take your advice on him.

"Now, Barbara," Kathy went on, very seriously. "One more thing, very important."

"Yes?"

"Next time we have dinner, it's got to be La Grenouille." I laughed. "Absolutely! You've got a deal."

Mitchell, as it turned out, was a whole different story. He was short and slightly round—not fat at all, but just approaching the pleasantly plump—and there was an air of mischief about him. He was *very* cute.

That mischievous quality shone through immediately the first time I called him. "Oh, *yes,*" he said, "yes, yes, yes, indeed. Paul told me lots about you, and I can't wait to meet you and see if we can't get your financial situation put in the proper order."

"I do need help straightening these things out, but it's hard for me to get away during the day."

"Well, Miss Ignoto, how about lunch? Sometimes a *lot* can be accomplished during a good working lunch."

"I, uh, I really can't take too long a lunch hour right now. Maybe sometime later when we've made a good start on my accounts, but for now maybe it would be better if we met in the evening so we'll have enough time to discuss things."

"Excellent, Miss Ignoto, excellent. As a single man, I have many evenings free, so any day that's convenient for you—at about seven o'clock?"

"How about tonight?"

"Wonderful!" he said, and gave me the address.

Mitchell lived in one of those modern high-rises on the First Avenue singles' strip. The apartment was a one-bedroom sorely in need of a woman's touch—or a maid's touch, or somebody's. There were clothes scattered around, books and records practically crying out to be put away, and an unmade bed. But it was clean, and the disarray somehow had a homey feel to it. I felt my maternal instincts starting to emerge.

Mitchell was barefoot and wearing jeans and an old plaid shirt, and even though he was not at all good-looking there was something appealing and cuddlesome about him. He asked me what I would like to drink. "I have Tropicana; I have Sacramento tomato juice, which isn't as good as it used to be since they started making it from concentrate—do you know a really good tomato juice?—and Heineken and Beck's and a few jugs of California plonk. And Perrier. And *lots* of ice cubes."

"Actually, Mitchell, since I just had dinner, I could use something stronger to help it all digest. If you've got some kind of brandy or liqueur, that would be great."

Mitchell looked perturbed. He went into the kitchen.

"Hmmm. I really must try to get my hard-stuff act together. Let's see . . . here's a bottle of sherry that's been here since I moved in, so it must be properly aged. It's not really strong, of course, but it has more alcohol than the wine."

"That's fine. Will you join me?"

"Why not? It's before dinner for me, but I guess sherry's main claim to fame is before dinner anyway. Cheers."

We drank; the sherry was just barely passable. I said, "Mitch—can I call you Mitch, it just seems more natural—"

"Of course. Please," with a shrug that said, no formality whatsoever, please.

"Mitch, what do you like?"

He beamed. "Ah. My tastes in sex are almost as uneducated as my taste in beverages. These married guys want special stuff that they can't get at home, but me, I can't get much of anything at home, so I'm not so demanding." He broke into a wonderful leer. "But, Barbara, I am very open to suggestions."

I laughed. He was delightful. "Well, there's what's called half-and-half. That's good for starters." I had picked up these expressions from Kathy, and although they still sounded a bit vulgar to me, they were so apt that I got used to them very quickly.

"Half-and-half? Not like in the pub joke?"

"No, I don't think so. What's the pub joke?"

"Ah. A drunk goes to a pub in a small English town at three in the morning and bangs on the door. The couple who own the pub live upstairs, and the banging wakes them up. The man sticks his head out the window and says, 'Go away, mate. We're closed. We're trying to sleep.'

" 'I wants me half-and-half,' the drunk says.

" 'I told you, we're closed. Come back tomorrow.'

" 'No, I wants me half-and-half now.'

" 'All right, just a minute,' and he goes and gets the chamber pot and pours it over the drunk's head and says, 'There's yer half-and-half, mate. It's half the old lady's and half mine.' "

I loved it. "Mitch, you're too much. No, half-and-half is much less kinky than that—it's a blow job and then a fuck."

"Sold! Let's do it!"

We went into the bedroom and got undressed. I wanted to ask Mitch for some foreplay for me, but I didn't know whether he was ready for that yet and thought it could wait for next time. I started sucking his cock, and he was so hot that he shot a gigantic load after only a few seconds. It was obvious that he hadn't had any sex for a long time.

"Wow," he said. "I've got to see you more often."

I wasn't sure what he meant—that it was so good or that he realized he wasn't getting enough. But I felt so at ease with him that I thought I could just be open and lay it all out on the table.

"Mitch, I want to see you a lot. But you need a girl friend too. It's like if you let yourself get too hungry, when you finally eat you can't really enjoy it and you wolf it down too fast. You need me for variety, for the strange stuff and"—I didn't want to put it so brutally as to say, "for me to teach you"—"for me to, to try to widen your horizons."

"You mean to teach me. Good idea. I'd like that. And the girl friend is a good idea too. But when you look like me, that's not so easy."

"But that's not true! You don't have to look like Robert Redford—looks aren't really that important. You're fun to be with, and you've got a great sense of humor, and that counts for more, believe me. Do you get out of this apartment that much? Do you go places? You're right here in the middle of all these singles' joints."

"Yeah, you're right. I don't get out enough—I guess I don't try enough. But you can get discouraged, you know? After you get rejected a few hundred times, you kind of lose your ambition."

"Well, maybe on second thought the singles' places aren't

such a good idea. You should try to meet someone who'll have enough time to get to know you and see that you're a wonderful person even though you aren't tall, dark, and handsome."

"But outside of work I don't meet that many women—and I don't think it's a good idea to get involved with someone at work."

"Mitch, this apartment is crawling with books and records. You go to book and record stores, right? Pick someone up there; if they're in the store they obviously share your interests—unless they've gone there just to get picked up. Ask them about a book or a record, or strike up a conversation. If a woman gets a chance to see what you're really like, she's going to like you, I guarantee it. And you're not *un*attractive physically—you're actually kinda cute. And you bring out the maternal instinct."

Mitch looked at me and gave me a sweet, sad smile. "The ones I meet that I really like, they're unattainable for one reason or another. Like you. Because you're so *open* and real. Most women aren't open; they're distant and manipulative—with me they are, anyway. So, I really like you, I mean—well, you know what I mean. But this is just business, right? And I wonder about that, you know? You're such a wonderful woman, and you are so open, why do you do this? Do you really like it?"

"Ah, Mitch, I love it and I hate it. Or I don't even know whether I love or hate it."

He frowned and looked mystified. "What do you mean?"

"Mitch, how much do you make?"

"Forty-four."

"Forty-four thousand a year. So you don't worry about money, right? You don't even think about it."

"No. You ever read James Baldwin?"

"No," I said. "I know who he is, but I've never read him."

"He wrote something very profound. He said that money

is like sex—when you have it you don't think about it, and when you don't have it you don't think about anything else."

"Perfect. Exactly. That's just what I'm trying to say. You don't think about money, because you have it—you have enough, more than enough. You know how much I make? Eighteen thousand a year. You know what it's like to live on that in New York City? So far as that goes, I love this, because it solves my problems. I don't have to *worry* all the time about how I'm going to pay for this, and about how if I get this I won't be able to afford that, and how I'm going to get by, and whether I can borrow some more, and how I'm going to pay back all my debts. That's a *horrible* feeling. And the other reason I love it is that I meet fantastic new people—you and some other guys. So why do I hate it? Because these can't be *real* friendships. The money and the relationships work against each other. And that bothers me, but I don't know how to handle it."

Mitch looked uncomfortable. "Well," he said hesitantly, "they could be real friendships if you wanted them to be, couldn't they?"

I slumped back and gave a great sigh. He had really hit the nail on the head. "I suppose so. But then where would that leave me? Seeing my boyfriend and three or four other guys? When would I have time to go to work and sleep? And what would happen to the solution to my money problems?"

Mitch nodded sadly. "I see. There isn't any solution, is there?"

"No kidding; tell me about it. There sure isn't."

Suddenly Mitch seemed to brighten; I could almost see the light bulb turning on above his head. "Barbara, I guess Ignoto isn't your real name, but are you really Italian?"

"Half. My father's Italian; my mother's Irish."

"So you're Catholic, right? You were brought up in the church?"

"Yeah. But so what?"

"But I mean, doesn't it get to you? Don't you feel that doing this is wrong?"

"No, no. I never really believed all that. I never took it seriously. I did most of it just to please my parents. My favorite quote of all time is from that woman in Italy that some reporter asked about the Pope's latest statement on birth control, and she said, 'He no play the game, he no make the rules.' I believe in God, but I don't like organized religion in the first place, and I think Catholicism is mainly a big scam."

"I know what you mean. And I agree with you a hundred percent. I just thought it might be a problem for you."

"No way. And even if I did basically believe, I don't think this is wrong. I don't think making love outside of marriage is wrong. I think love and sex are wonderful things to have —God-given things, I would even say."

"Barbara, call me soon, okay? Meanwhile, how much do I owe you?"

"Fifty bucks. And I will call you soon."

Mitch gave me the cash; no envelope this time, but it didn't bother me at all, because I thought of his money as a tuition fee. I was going to teach him how to please a woman and how to be a real man. Professor Ignoto herself; maybe I would get a chair at Fordham. Sexuality 101. Professor Ignoto. Lab fee three hundred dollars. Well, maybe not at Fordham.

It was almost ten by the time I got home, and I was planning to go right to bed, but Kathy called, wanting to know what was happening.

"I saw Mitch tonight. The accountant."

"How was it?"

"Kind of wonderful-terrible. I didn't enjoy it physically at all—he's not a good lover like Paul and Tony. As a matter of fact, I don't think he has the faintest idea what he's doing, because he seems to be kind of a loser with women. But he's lots of fun otherwise, and I think I'm going to get a big kick out of teaching him about sex."

"Why not? He doesn't sound like my type, but you have fun. I've got another guy for you, if you want."

I laughed, but with more irony and resignation than humor. "Why not? Maybe I'll end up doing this full-time. Who is it now?"

"Oh, come on, Barbara, don't sound like that. You don't have to see him tomorrow, you know—you can take a week off. Anyway, his name is Arnie, he's a newspaperman, and he's a very sweet guy."

"I don't know whether I really need another sweet guy—I think I may be ready for a son-of-a-bitch bastard, but as usual my curiosity is going to get the better of me. What's his number?"

Kathy gave me the details and said, "You know, I still want to go to Grenouille. You made it sound so wonderful."

"You don't have to talk me into it. I'd love to go back there again. I'll ask Tony to make us a reservation."

"Good idea. Any night at all is fine with me. And come to think of it, why didn't Tony ever take *me* to Grenouille? That bastard."

"That's obvious, Kathy; he knew you weren't so delicate and didn't need such a gentle introduction to these naughty activities. And of course, I'm much more beautiful."

"Oh, yeah, sure. Get us a good table at Grenouille, you bitch, or I'm going to steal your boyfriend away from you."

"You're welcome to him! Can you do it tomorrow?"

Kathy chuckled. "I don't want sloppy seconds—I'll wait for juicy thirds. Call me tomorrow."

"Sure. Goodnight." And I fell into bed.

I was very curious to meet Arnie, but I decided I needed a week off, and since it was getting to be the bad time of the month for me anyway, that worked out fine. I started thinking about getting a new apartment; I had had my fill of Amsterdam Avenue, and I could afford something better now. I wanted something on the East Side; it's more peaceful and serene over there and the neighborhoods are better all around. The problem is that it's so hard to find an apartment in Manhattan, and I didn't have time for a long search. I thought of asking Paul or Tony to help, but then I realized that I didn't want them to know where I lived. Then it struck me that since Arnie worked for a newspaper, he could probably get the Sunday real estate ads for me in advance, and that would at least give me a jump on everyone else. I made up my mind that I would call him first thing after my week's "vacation."

I phoned him on my lunch hour, but they told me he started work at two, so I called again at about five thirty after I left work. He sounded very distracted and busy but nice enough.

"Barbara, I can't talk now, but I get off about nine thirty. Can we meet somewhere for a drink about ten?"

"Ouch. That's kind of late for me."

"Okay, well, I'm off Wednesdays and Thursdays. We can make it earlier then. Can you call me at around three on Tuesday?"

"Will do."

"Okay, 'bye."

I called back Tuesday at the stroke of three and we set up a dinner date for seven o'clock Wednesday at Christ Cella, another famous restaurant that I'd heard of but had never been to. I began to be afraid that although these dinners were a wonderful fringe benefit for me, I might end up weighing three hundred pounds. I was going to have to cut down on those lunchtime yogurts.

Christ Cella was a very plain-looking steakhouse, but in one way it had the best decor in the world: it was full of men —mostly young, good-looking men with an air of wealth. There were only a few other women in the place, and they were almost all stunners. It struck me that when you go to a steakhouse or a French restaurant, those places that serve huge portions of rich food full of fat and cholesterol, you see wonderfully healthy-looking, vibrant, sexy people, but when you go to a health food restaurant you see wizened, frail-looking basket cases or fat people who look like they're almost at death's door. That had to mean something.

Arnie was already there when I arrived, sitting at a table for four in a corner of the back room, drinking a bloody mary—or maybe a virgin, let's not jump to conclusions—and smoking a Camel. He had thinning brown hair and kind of craggy, weatherbeaten good looks. He was wearing an olive blazer and a light gray button-down shirt, and altogether he looked as if he should be smoking a pipe instead of cigarettes.

We made small talk for a while and ordered what Arnie suggested: a Caesar salad to share, a double steak medium rare topped with garlic, hash-brown potatoes and sautéed onions, with a bottle of Nuit St.-Georges. The food was out of this world, and I said, "You know, I'm getting to know some terrific restaurants in this life, and I love it."

"You've met the right guy. Dining out is my biggest consolation, and I'm always in the market for a companion as charming as you."

He had been kind of distant so far, but I was intrigued by him and was determined to open him up.

"Consolation? Do you really need to be consoled? And surely you mean the *second*-biggest consolation?"

Arnie smiled. "You've got a point there. I guess I need to be consoled because I'm kind of semimarried."

"Semimarried? You mean you're in the process of getting a divorce?"

"No. I kind of wish it had reached that stage, because then the thing would be getting resolved, but we're separated. Every once in a while we make kind of an attempt to get back together, but it doesn't work. But we just can't bring ourselves to the point of getting divorced and calling it quits once and for all."

"Complicating factors? Children?"

Arnie nodded. "A son—Willie. He's thirteen. He lives with my wife in our house in Rockland County, and I've got an apartment on West End Avenue. I visit Willie once in a while, but not as often as I'd like."

"And you're lonely."

"Yes. I haven't been able to meet anyone new that I really like."

"So you see Kathy. And now me. Does that help?"

He looked into my eyes and smiled an ironic smile. "Consolation. It's a cliché that newspapermen drink, and the reason it became a cliché is that it's basically true. But I stick to my virgin marys and wine, and I guess you and Kathy are my escape. Much better than liquor, don't you think?"

"Definitely. But is it as good as finding a new relationship? Why don't you do that?"

"Partly because I still cling to hopes of settling things with my wife. When I do meet someone new, I compare her to my wife and she comes out a very poor second, and I think, What's the use?"

"I'm tempted to say you have to keep trying, but I guess that sounds awfully lame."

"Someday I have to decide to get myself together. In the meantime, I drift and try to enjoy life as much as possible. Now, how about you? Why do you do this? Why don't you just live a normal life?"

"I think I can do both. And I've gotten hooked on this— interesting men, good times, fine restaurants, a second income. The problem is, there's more emotional involvement than I expected—I thought it would be just wham, bam, thank you, ma'am."

"Anyone who wants that can just go to a regular hooker. I think you'll learn to distance yourself from it by just the right amount."

61

"I hope so. We'll see. In the meantime, I'm having lots of fun."

"Barbara, until you've had cheesecake here you don't know what fun is."

"I'll burst. But I'll split a piece with you. And then I'd like to tell you about my housing problem."

"It's a deal on both counts—you can move in with me tonight. Coffee or café filtre?"

"Filtre, if there's no espresso. And actually, I was thinking of a new apartment just for me. Can you get me a jump on the Sunday real estate section?"

"Easy. You can pick it up at lunchtime tomorrow. I'm off, but I'll have someone leave it for you in the lobby. Just ask the guard—there'll be an envelope with your name on it."

"Great. I love envelopes."

It took him a second to get it, then he smiled at me conspiratorially. He was right about the cheesecake, and the café filtre was strong enough to make that giant meal seem to magically disappear and to keep you awake until the weekend—but delicious. I drank three cups of it, and I felt ready for anything.

Arnie and I took a cab to his apartment on West End Avenue, and we started fooling around in the taxi; I guess he just couldn't wait or couldn't resist me. We were French kissing and he put his hand under my skirt and caressed my thighs, then he slowly, teasingly moved his hand up and stroked my pussy through my panties. I was already getting wet, and I decided to return the favor; I stroked his hard-on through his pants. Then he went inside my panties and finger-fucked me gently. I unzipped his fly and rubbed his cock through his shorts. I was trying to get my hand inside when the voice finally got through to us.

"Sir? Sir? Which corner, sir?"

"Oh, uh, the far corner is fine, thanks," Arnie said with what I thought was an admirable degree of composure. We scrambled to get ourselves together and the driver, bless his heart, kept a straight face. Arnie handed him a ten-dollar bill and said, "Thanks a lot," and opened the door for me.

"Thank *you*, sir. Have a pleasant evening."

I burst out laughing. "How nice he was! Let's wait to see if he stops to wipe off his back seat."

Arnie grabbed me and shoved me playfully toward his building. "Come on, wiseass."

We behaved ourselves in the elevator even though we were the only passengers; Arnie restricted himself to feeling up my ass.

He took my hand and led me straight to the bedroom. He tossed his jacket onto a chair and unbuttoned his shirt and said, "I must warn you that Kathy has gotten me very spoiled."

I smiled at him teasingly and took off my skirt. "Really? How so?"

Arnie looked at my legs appreciatively. "A tongue bath. Everywhere."

I was starting to feel like Little Miss Cocktease. "If you give me enough time, I think I can even find some new places. And then?"

"I like it doggie style. Nice and deep that way." His tone was taking on a frantic edge that made me very excited. I started to unbutton my blouse but Arnie said, "Take your panties off first."

I took them off and lay down on the bed and spread my legs and started fingering myself and stroking my clit. Arnie stared at me entranced while he took off his pants. His hard-on looked as if it were going to rip his shorts open. I took off my blouse while he took off his shorts; his cock was huge and beautiful and throbbing like mad.

Arnie lay down next to me, and I started by licking his ears and his neck. Then I started licking and sucking his armpit, and he moaned and said, "Yeah." I wanted to stroke his cock but he was so hot I was afraid that if I did he would come right then and there, so I stroked his balls and his asshole. I sucked first one armpit, then the other, then did the same with his nipples. I was moving down to suck his balls, but Arnie couldn't wait and turned over on all fours. I started eating his asshole, alternately licking and sticking my tongue in and sucking, and meanwhile I was stroking his balls lightly with my fingertips. Arnie was going out of his mind, moaning and groaning, and I could sense that he couldn't wait for me to start sucking his cock but was loving this so much that he didn't want it to end. I sucked his ass for a long time, and finally he pulled away and turned over and motioned me into a sixty-nine position. I put my pussy over his face and licked up and down his cock while he sucked my cunt and clit, and I took his cock in my mouth and sucked him slowly. Arnie was so hot, he could take only a few seconds of this, and he took his mouth away from me and said, "Okay." I got on all fours and let my ass hang over the edge of the bed. Arnie stood behind me and eased his cock into my pussy. He was right; he could get in very deep this way, and he thrust very slowly, going in as deep as he could and then giving a little extra poke just for good measure. It felt tremendous, and I was giving little moans and saying, "Oh!" Then I discovered that he liked to talk during sex to make himself even hotter than he already was. "You need a cock in your mouth now to complete the picture."

"Ummm. I'd like that. And you need a tongue up your ass."

"Yes—yes, yes. You want to do a threesome some time?"

"I'd love to. You ever do one with Kathy?"

"No, not yet—but I'd like to. And I'd love to see you with another woman."

"I want to try that—oh, Arnie, fuck me harder now."

We had gotten ourselves into a frenzied state, and Arnie started pounding me really hard and came frantically; in this position I could really *feel* him coming. He stayed in me for a long time, and there was a delicious afterglow. Finally we both collapsed back onto the bed, with me dripping his come onto his sheets, but I'm sure he didn't care.

I gave Arnie a deep soul kiss and said, "You're so fine and *freaky.*"

He laughed. "You too. And you really want to get into a few scenes?"

"I'd love to—I'm at the point now where I want to try everything. I think we should arrange for me and Kathy to do you together. One in front and one in back—whatever you want."

"Would you like to make it with Kathy?"

"Wow. I don't know whether I'm ready for that. We're too close, you know? I am curious about going with another woman, but that's just on the fantasy level—maybe when the time came I'd get cold feet."

Arnie laughed. "You don't strike me as the cold-feet type. But let's just see what happens. You want to talk to Kathy about our threesome, or do you want me to?"

"I think it's better if I do. You're not in any hurry, are you?"

"Not too—anticipating and looking forward to it will be satisfying in itself. But let's not wait too long."

"No—and let's not wait too long to see each other again."

"Barbara, I'd be delighted to make it every week. Next Wednesday—and every Wednesday."

"You've got a date. I may have to take off one week a month, you know?"

"We can work around that—if you don't mind."

"I hadn't thought of that—there are alternatives, aren't there? Sure, I'll give it a try."

"Great. And let me know what happens with the apartment."

We said our good-byes, and I headed home with visions of my new apartment alternating in my head with visions of threesomes. Arnie had really turned me on in more ways than one.

The next day on my lunch hour I went straight to the newspaper office and got the Sunday real estate section. I bought a fruit salad with cottage cheese on my way back to the office and sat at my desk eating and circling ads that looked promising. One of the other girls in the office stopped by and saw what I was doing and said, "Barbara, you're looking for an apartment?"

"Yeah. I've had my fill of the West Side, Sue. Now that I'm getting old, I want something real quiet and peaceful."

"I know of a place that's going to be opening up near Second Avenue. A friend of mine is giving it up—it's a small studio, but nice. Would that interest you?"

"Would that interest me! Is the Pope Catholic?"

Sue laughed. She was a soulful-looking brunette with a great ass and nice legs. Why was I noticing these things now? "The only problem is that it's expensive—it's six hundred dollars."

I winced, convincingly. "Ouch. That's more than double what I'm paying now. But most of these in the paper are that much or more, so I guess I'm just gonna have to be rent-poor."

Sue smiled. "Join the crowd, Barbara. Or find yourself a sugar daddy."

We worked out an arrangement for the apartment, and it turned out that I had to give both Sue's girl friend and the super a month's rent as key money. I didn't think that was at all unfair, since they could easily have gotten a thousand bucks each as key money and were doing a favor for a friend of a friend. But I just didn't have the twelve hundred dollars. Then it struck me that I had several good prospects for an interest-free loan.

I called Kathy. "Look, I've got a good line on a new apartment, but I need twelve hundred dollars in key money. I think you can help me arrange to borrow it, so if you want to have dinner tonight I thought we could discuss it."

"Great. And I may have some good news for us. Can't talk about it now."

We made a date for our old standby in Little Italy, and I spent the afternoon wondering what Kathy's news was.

I got to the restaurant first, and when Kathy arrived she was bursting with excitement.

"Kathy, something tells me that the good news has come through."

"Yes! We got it! Grenouille! Tony's going to *take* us—both of us—on Monday. Cancel all other appointments!"

I laughed. "Kathy, that's great, but calm down. It is a terrific place, but it's not better than sex. Maybe *as* good, though, come to think of it. And speaking of sex, what do we do about after dinner? Toss a coin?"

Kathy raised her eyebrows and gave me such a great look of mock seriousness that I giggled. "That's something we have to talk about, my girl," she said. "I have the *distinct* feeling that Tony would like a double helping, if you know what I mean. Are you ready for that?"

"Why not? I'll try anything once. It sounds like fun. And it's a good excuse to drink a lot of wine at dinner—that'll help get us in the mood."

"We'll see what happens. We'll keep an open mind. From what you told me about that restaurant, I'd risk almost anything to go there. Just thinking about it is making me hungry. Let's order, and then we can talk about your apartment loan."

We ordered arugula salads and saltimbocca and a bottle of Soave, and I told Kathy I thought one of our guys would lend me the twelve hundred dollars and asked her which one she thought I should approach first.

She shook her head. "No good. They won't give it to you, and they'll be put off by your asking. Barbara, you've got to get it through your head that although these guys are friends, they're not *friend* friends, you know? These are business relationships. And that reminds me of something I've been meaning to talk to you about. How much are you charging?"

"Fifty dollars."

"For everything? No matter what you do?"

"Well, yeah." I didn't tell her that Tony had given me a hundred dollars on our first date, because I hadn't asked for any specific amount and he had just voluntarily given it to me. So I figured that didn't count.

Kathy shook her head again. "That's the wrong way. You remember when I first told you I was doing this I explained about the different prices for different things?"

"Yeah, but I thought for me, since it's just the beginning for me—"

"But the beginning is over now. Have you discussed prices with any of them?"

"No. I haven't really wanted to, I guess. It just seems so—so crass and kind of—kind of whorish, you know?"

Another shake of the head. "Barbara, that's just what I mean about remembering that this is basically a business. They're not going to be offended; they're all in business, and they know all about deals and negotiating, and they realize very well that this is a deal. I'm not going to tell you what to charge, but it shouldn't be the same if you do everything as it is for a straight fuck."

"You're right. I'll think of some ladylike way to bring it up. And as for the apartment money, I guess I should just go to the bank. Now that I'm going to adjust my fees, I won't have any trouble paying it back."

Kathy reached down for her purse and took out an envelope and handed it to me. "Barbara, here's a check; I'm lending you the money. I can spare it. You can pay me back whenever you get a chance."

I looked at the check and then at her and then put it in my bag. "Kathy, thank you—thanks a lot. That's terrific. If we didn't already have an invite, I'd take *you* to Grenouille."

Kathy smiled and toasted me with her wineglass. "That's

okay—on second thought, I may take a raincheck. Now, tell me again about their menu."

We had a nice dinner, talking about food, and that night I called Arnie and Michael and told them about the apartment. The next day at work, I told Sue I could pay the key money over the weekend and made arrangements to take the apartment on the first of the month. Michael would help me move, and my landlord would be delighted to let me break my lease because it meant he could jack up the rent on my place. I felt wonderfully happy; everything was working out, I'd have a much better place to live, and my life seemed to be taking big turns for the better. And to top it all off, I could look forward to another fantastic dinner on Monday —and a fantastic evening of entertainment.

When I got up Monday morning, I decided to dress for the occasion; even though the dinner date wasn't until six thirty and I get off work at five, I didn't feel like running home to change and then having to rush back downtown again. I knew it would mean a lot of teasing at work, but I put on a black cocktail dress with a slit skirt, a pearl necklace (fake of course, but nice-looking), and high heels.

"Ooh, wow, guess who has a heavy date tonight," Sue said when I got to work.

"Beyond your wildest dreams," I said haughtily, smiling to myself. Little did she know how true that was.

"Celebrating your new apartment?"

I smiled at her warmly. "Of course. And thanks again."

Otherwise the day dragged, and I had more than an hour to kill after work. I toyed with the idea of calling Paul or Mitch for a quickie at five thirty, but then I decided that would be idiotic—twice in one night would be too much, I wouldn't really be in shape for the dinner, and it would be a rush. *Do something constructive,* I said to myself.

Suddenly I remembered that it was Monday and Bloomingdale's was open late. I could go there and look for things for the apartment until six fifteen or so and then walk to the restaurant.

I was looking at carpeting and thinking about how nice it would be to get some of that deep plushy stuff that feels so great to walk on barefoot, when I felt someone staring at me. I glanced up and saw this incredible hunk looking at me and smiling. He was about six feet tall, with smoky gray-blue eyes and long straw-colored hair that fell over his forehead. I don't usually undress guys in my mind, but all of a sudden I had visions of him naked on a bed, his chest sweaty and with just enough of that light hair. Why did this have to happen *now?*

"Hello," he said, giving me a smile of about ten thousand watts. "You know anything about carpeting?"

"Actually, no. But I was hoping maybe you did, because I think I know what I want but I don't even know what it's called."

"Uh-oh. We're not going to be any help to each other, because I don't know the first thing about carpeting."

"Well, uh, do you have any idea what kind you want?"

He gave me that smile again. "Can I tell you the truth?"

"Sure."

"What I want here is not carpeting. I have plain wooden parquet floors and I like them that way. I've been following you since you walked in the door at Fifty-ninth Street."

"Oh. Well—I'm flattered. I'm also Barbara."

"Steven."

"Delighted to meet you, Steven. Really. Now can I tell *you* the truth?"

"Please."

"I have a date for tonight. I have a boyfriend. I don't give new acquaintances my telephone number. But I'd love to get to know you, and if you want to give me your number I'll call you as soon—"

He was writing already. He handed me a business card that said STEVEN C. GARSON. PHOTOGRAPHY and had both the printed telephone number and the one he had just written. "The first number is for business and is linked to an answering service. This one is for friends and has an answering machine. So, Barbara, call either one, anytime—but do call, please. Don't just disappear from my life."

"I won't—I mean, I will. I mean, I will call but I won't disappear. But I may not be able to call for a couple of weeks, because there's a lot going on in my life right now, but I will definitely call."

He shrugged and smiled. "I'll wait. Not patiently, but I'll wait."

I held out my hand, and he took it lightly. "I'll be worth the wait," I said, and walked away with a little wave. That incredible sunrise smile again, this time with a touch of humor and delight. What a stunner! I could have made love to him right then and there.

I walked out of the store in a kind of daze and started to walk to La Grenouille. A lot going on in my life indeed! When it rains, it pours.

I walked down Lex and across Fifty-seventh Street and down Fifth. I've always loved Fifty-seventh Street, a wide boulevard that goes from one end of the island to the other and is lined, especially on the East Side, with chic, classy stores. And on this beautiful May evening it seemed more entrancing than ever. I passed the Dorchester Hotel and Le Chantilly, with that wonderful long white canopy and the white curtains in the window; the door was open, and I got a glimpse of the maître d'hotel greeting a handsome couple and the roast cart with its big silver cover. At Park, I crossed to the uptown side of the street so I could look into the windows of Baccarat and Porthault, and when I turned down Fifth, it was more of the same: Mark Cross and the St. Regis Hotel and Gucci—they all seemed to perfume the air with a sense of wealth and ease and well-being. Everything seemed right with the world, and when I walked into La Grenouille, the glowing lamps and the flowers and that fantastic cold table brought my enchantment to a perfect climax.

"Ah, Miss Eeeg-noh-too, *bon soir.* Your party is already here." Only this charming maître d' could pronounce *Ignoto* as a French name!—and then make me feel terrific by saying "your party," as if I was the hostess. And I was still in awe of the seemingly magical ability of the best New York maîtres d'hotel to remember your name after having seen you only once.

Kathy and Tony were deep in conversation and had already started on a bottle of Taittinger champagne. Kathy looked absolutely stunning in a low-cut strapless dress. They looked up and said hello and they seemed not only glad but also relieved to see me. I would have loved to know what their conversation had been about—but maybe I'd find out soon enough.

The waiter poured me a glass of the champagne, and its elegant, dry, complex deliciousness heightened the comfortable high that champagne always gives me. We ordered dinner—caviar "to go with the champagne," as Tony put it, and then asparagus hollandaise as a second course. The captain suggested softshell crabs, a special that night not on the menu; Kathy had them with garlic and tomatoes, and Tony ordered them meunière—lightly floured and sautéed in butter. I had such fond memories of the Dover sole that I couldn't resist having it again, grilled with a mustard sauce. But we all shared and got to taste a bit of everything. Kathy loves food even more than I do, if that's possible, and she was positively beside herself with pleasure and excitement over being at Grenouille and tasting these incredible dishes. Tony ordered a bottle of Montrachet, and although I had silent fears that it wouldn't be enough for three people, on top of the champagne it turned out to be just enough.

We had a delightful time, talking mostly about food and wine and restaurants. I ate slower and slower as I got toward the end, to try to make it last as long as possible, and we decided to take a break and smoke before dessert.

"What do you recommend, Tony?" Kathy asked. "Those raspberries we saw on the way in looked irresistible, but what else is there?"

"Ah—there are soufflés. Any flavor you want—Grand Marnier, chocolate, lemon, anything. And floating island and chocolate mousse and fruit tarts and of course sherbets and ice cream."

Kathy looked agonized. "I can't decide between the raspberries and a soufflé."

"Have both!" Tony said. "I've found many a time that you don't have to choose between two wonderful things— you can have them both. At the same time."

Tony couldn't help chuckling, he was so pleased with himself. Kathy and I looked at him and at each other and giggled; we were both slightly high anyway from all the champagne and wine.

"Oh?" Kathy said coquettishly. "Well, if you're sure that's really true, Tony. I'll have the raspberries and part of whatever soufflé you and Barbara want."

Tony looked at me and said, "Grand Marnier? Almond? Strawberry? Lemon?"

"Strawberry and lemon both sound wonderful. Does the Victor Principle apply to soufflés too?"

"Does it ever!" he said, and he ordered a big plate of raspberries for everyone and a strawberry-and-lemon soufflé.

After the café filtre, Tony said, "Cognac at my place, ladies. And how about a long slow walk to help us recover from dinner?"

"The walk sounds great," I said. "And the cognac sounds great. And then do we have *specific* plans, or do we just see what develops?"

Kathy laughed. "Actually, Barbara, Tony and I have a confession to make to you. We were discussing this before you got here, and we settled on the fee and talked about some possible—uh, scenarios. And one of them is, well"—Kathy paused and took a drag on her cigarette and then used it to light another one; I had never seen her chain-smoke before—"something that you and I are probably not ready for. But aside from that, we decided on a combination of anything goes and seeing what develops." She thought for a second and then laughed. "If that makes any sense."

Tony just smiled and looked at both of us. I said, "It makes fine sense to me. As a matter of fact, I would say you put it very well—wouldn't you, Tony?"

"Couldn't have said it any better myself—couldn't have said it half as well."

I was pretty sure I knew what Kathy meant. Tony wanted to see Kathy and me make it with each other, but we weren't ready for that—boy, we sure weren't. I certainly wasn't. But aside from that, fine, and I could hardly wait to see what would happen.

Even so, I was very glad of the walk. The evening was still lovely, with none of that chill in the air that you sometimes get on a May night, and we strolled slowly up Fifth Avenue all the way to Seventy-second Street, then doubled back and over to Tony's place.

Tony poured cognac for us, and we sat there sipping and making small talk. There was a slight sense of unease in the air, a kind of How-do-we-start? feeling, but also a delicious sense of anticipation. I had never done a threesome before, not even on an amateur basis, but I felt very curious and ready for this next initiation rite of my new life. Finally Tony got up and went into the bedroom and said, "Whenever you're ready, ladies. If you'd like more cognac, please do help yourselves."

Kathy and I looked at each other, took a few more sips, and followed Tony into the bedroom. I was still feeling just slightly uneasy about the whole thing, but when I walked into the bedroom and saw Tony lying on the bed naked with a gigantic hard-on, lust and excitement took over. I sat down

on the bed and started licking Tony's cock without even
bothering to get undressed. Kathy sat down by Tony's pillow on the other side of the bed, and he pulled her dress
down and started massaging her breasts. She gave a satisfied
little "ummm," then took off the dress and her panties and
lowered herself over Tony's face. He sucked her pussy while
I slowly sucked his cock, and after a minute or so he lifted
her off and pulled away from me. Then he stood up on the
bed with his back to me. At first I couldn't figure out what
he was doing, but then he said, "Okay, switch! Barbara, you
take the back and Kathy the front." I knelt behind him and
sucked his ass while Kathy knelt in front and licked his balls
and then sucked his cock. Tony moaned like he was in sev-
enth heaven and murmured, "Oh. That's so beautiful." He
came after a while, and that was that.

I was a little disappointed. This was my first threesome,
and from my point of view it was no big deal. I could well
understand how being blown and rimmed at the same time
had been the fulfillment of a big fantasy for Tony, but I felt
frustrated and unsatisfied. Then I reminded myself that satisfying me wasn't the point of these dates, that I was getting
paid to provide the satisfaction and couldn't always expect
to be turned on as I had been the first few times. And the
point was driven home when, after we said goodnight and
exclaimed how we really must do this again soon, I opened
my envelope while we were standing in the hall waiting for
the elevator and found three fifty-dollar bills. "Kathy, you
drive a great bargain—thanks!"

"That's okay—but put it away. We've got to be cool; there
may be someone on the elevator."

But I was still feeling horny and unsatisfied, and when
Kathy said she had to run to see her boyfriend, that gave me
an idea. Michael really wasn't one for spur-of-the-moment
meetings, but he wouldn't turn me away either. When I
called, I got his answering machine, but since he sometimes

leaves it on when he's home so he can screen calls, I said, "Michael, it's Barbara. Are you there? Michael?" but there was no answer.

Damn, I thought. I was just not in the mood to go back to my dump on Amsterdam Avenue; as a matter of fact, I could hardly wait for the next few days to pass until I could move out. It was just ten o'clock, but that was too late to call Paul. But Arnie!—it would be a perfect time for Arnie. I was going to see him Wednesday, but I wanted to see him so badly then, right then, that I would even make it for free, as a bonus night, if I had to. I remembered that he got off work at nine thirty, so if he had gone home he might just be there.

I called, and I was in luck.

"Arnie. It's Barbara. How are you? Can I come over? I'd love to see you."

"You mean right now?"

"Yeah—in about twenty minutes."

"Uh—sure. That'll give me just enough time to get organized. We still have our date for Wednesday, right?"

"Absolutely. Is that too much Barbara in one week?"

"Oh, no, not at all. This is a very pleasant surprise. I was just worried you might be switching from Wednesday. See you in about twenty minutes."

"Great! 'Bye."

I found a cab right away and made it to Arnie's place in about ten minutes. I didn't want to break in on him early, but neither did I feel like wandering around to kill ten minutes, so I called again from a pay phone on the corner and asked if I could come right up, and he said sure.

He opened the door in his bathrobe and greeted me with a polite kiss, but I practically stuck my tongue down his throat and reached under the robe to caress his cock and balls.

"Wow! What's the occasion, Barbara? And what's the rush?"

"The answer to both questions is the same: I feel exceptionally horny." I was already getting undressed.

Arnie laughed. "Barbara, you need a boyfriend."

"He's not home. But I've got you. And you know something?" I said, getting rid of the last of my clothes and throwing my arms around him. "I think I'd rather have you anyway."

"I am flattered. And turned on."

We went into the bedroom and immediately got into a hot sixty-nine. I was kind of playing the aggressor, and Arnie went along with it. After we had eaten each other for a few minutes, I lifted my head and said, "Let's do an asshole sixty-nine," and we shifted around a bit so we could suck each other's assholes at the same time. This made me even more frantic than I already was. We did it for a long time, really getting into it, then went back to a regular sixty-nine. I was on top, with Arnie lying on the bed, and when I pulled away from him and turned around, he started to get up. I put my hand on his chest and gently pushed him back down on the bed. He grinned at me and helped me sit on his cock. I got his cock deep inside me, and we started moving together in a perfect rhythm. I leaned forward to suck his nipples and armpits, and when I did his cock seemed to go in even deeper. He started thrusting harder and faster, and I began to come. I could feel him exploding inside me, and I came again and again for what seemed a long time. I was lifted into a trance where space and time seemed to disappear. I stayed on top of Arnie, managing to hold his half-limp cock inside me and kissing him tenderly, until I managed to come back down into the world, then I got slowly off and lay down next to him.

"Wow. Arnie, you're wasting your time."

"*Wasting* it? There isn't any way I'd rather spend it."

"No, I mean you're wasting your time working for a newspaper. Or working at all. You're such a good lover you should just do that."

"Oh my God, she's trying to recruit me! Arnie and Barbara: couple will fulfill your wildest fantasies. Call any time, day or night. Only three hundred dollars for both."

I laughed. "Good idea! Put that ad in tomorrow, will you? I'm sure you can get us a discount."

"Seriously, Barbara, you're not half-bad yourself. I don't know how we're going to top this on Wednesday, but I was wondering if you'd like to go to a show."

"A play? I'd love to. I haven't been to the theater in a long time. Which one?"

"Any one you want."

"Really? But it's probably too late to get tickets for the ones I most want to see."

"Doesn't matter—I just call the press agent and ask for house tickets. One advantage of working for a newspaper. So take your pick."

"I'd love to see *A Chorus Line*. Oh, but I guess you must have already seen it."

"I have, but it's the kind you can easily enjoy twice or even three times. And how about dinner afterward—at Il Valletto?"

"After would make it too late for me—I've got to go to work Thursday morning, and I need my sleep. Just staying up so late tonight is going to leave me dragging ass tomorrow. It's been so worth it tonight, but twice in one week would be too much. But if you want to eat before the show—"

"You got it. Can you meet me at Wally's at six?"

"Oh, on Forty-ninth Street, right? I'll be there."

"Wonderful. And Barbara, is it okay if I pay you on Wednesday for tonight? This was unexpected, you know, and I don't have enough cash."

"Of course—sure. And since we're on the subject, I guess I should tell you that Kathy says I'm breaking union rules by charging fifty dollars all the time no matter what I do. So

I guess I'm going to adopt her schedule of fees. But not for tonight—I almost feel like I should pay *you* for tonight."

"Let's see—that'll be four dollars, please. No, that's fine— I should pay you the same as I pay Kathy—that's only fair. We'll see what happens Wednesday and settle up then."

I was relieved that Arnie had taken it so nicely. I could see that with the dinner and the show, he wanted to treat me like a regular friend, and I had been a little afraid that talking about the money might have spoiled that for him. But it became clear as I got to know him better that he had no problem in balancing out this kind of conflict in his mind. For one thing, he has loads of money; he makes an excellent salary and a lot of extra cash from freelance writing, and I think he gets some income from an inheritance. I don't know how much he gives his wife, but by now I had a rule of not asking anything about wives and not commenting on any family information that the guys did volunteer. But the more I saw how much Arnie loved taking me out to dinner and the theater, the more I understood that he viewed the money not so much as the price he had to pay for me but as the price for a friend who requires no real involvement and no commitment. This way he keeps total control of the relationship. And besides, he says, I'm much better in bed than most of the women he could get.

We had another delightful dinner at Wally's, a steakhouse with a semi-Italian menu. We both ate baked clams, superb steaks, and spinach sautéed in olive oil and garlic, with strawberries and whipped cream for dessert. Arnie and I talked about my life and life in general and my plans for the future. I told him that eventually I wanted to get married and have kids, but not until I was about thirty-two or thirty-three, and that right now I was having too much fun with my new double life.

"Enjoying it enough to want to meet someone else?"

"Oh, Arnie, that's one of my problems. I've got four regulars now, and at this point I think that's enough. Maybe *more* than enough. I guess if I wanted to, I could expand this to ten guys or a dozen or whatever—but I don't want to do that. I want to keep it under control, manageable, and I can't let it crowd out my regular life. But I'm always so curious and interested about meeting new guys. I would like to meet this man, if you recommend him, but I think that's got to be the end of it for now. Five is enough. If this guy wants to introduce me to his friends, the answer is going to be no."

"Sure—that's okay. Just say you're too busy and you can't. But I think you'll really like Jerry. He's a fascinating guy, and he knows this city inside out—he knows every club, every dive, every restaurant. You could have a lot of fun with him."

"Is he someone you work with?"

"No, he's a cab driver."

"A taxi driver? Wait a minute, now. I'm probably the least snobbish person in the world, and if Jerry is a friend of yours he's a friend of mine, but can he afford to do this?"

Arnie nodded vigorously. "Oh, yeah. He owns his own cab, he's single with no responsibilities, and he has a second line of work."

I laughed. "Then we have something in common! What's *his* other line?"

"He—he's a distributor of certain controlled substances."

"Oh—you mean, like a freelance pharmacist?"

"Perfect! Exactly—that's it. But not the really bad stuff— no smack or angel dust or anything like that. Just grass, coke, and speed."

"I don't know if I want to get involved with all that, but if you say he's okay, that's good enough for me. What's his number?"

Arnie gave me the telephone number and told me that Jerry usually worked from about four in the afternoon until four in the morning, so the best time to call him was around noon. Then we were off to see *A Chorus Line,* which I absolutely adored; my favorites were the tits-and-ass song and "What I Did for Love," both of which I could really relate to. Then we went back to Arnie's place and made good old-fashioned love in the missionary position—for us, it made a nice change! He gave me a hundred fifty for Monday and Wednesday, which was fine with me. It was a perfect evening, except for the fact that I didn't get to bed until about twelve thirty. But I found out later that Arnie got off early on Saturdays, so from then on that became our night for the theater.

I was a bit bushed on Thursday, and since I had made three hundred dollars in three days and had a lot of work to do to prepare for moving, I decided that Jerry and all the rest of them would have to wait until I was settled in my new apartment. Moving was less of a hassle than I expected, and the apartment was perfect for me—just big enough, very modern and comfortable, in a solid, classy neighborhood. And I had been able to get some of that really deep carpeting. That, of course, reminded me of Steven; I called up and got his answering machine and left a message: "I've been thinking about you but I still need a few more weeks. Patience, Steven, patience, please. It'll be *so* worth it." I felt a little guilty about teasing him with that last comment, but it was too late then; I couldn't erase the tape, and a second message would have just made things worse.

After I got myself squared away, I called Jerry.

He was very warm and friendly and told me that since he set his own hours, he could see me anytime but wanted to make a full-scale evening of it, with dinner and a club. Little did I know then what he meant by a club. I told him I didn't like to stay out late during the week but that Friday or Saturday would be fine, and we set up a date for Saturday. He asked me to meet him at eight o'clock at the Gloucester House, a restaurant with a reputation as the best fish place in town but incredibly expensive. It was obvious that my fears about Jerry's finances had been totally unfounded. But I was getting very spoiled in the restaurant department; it was getting so bad that I almost felt cheated that Paul and Mitch didn't feed me.

Jerry turned out to be just as nice as he'd sounded on the phone, and not bad-looking. He was thin, with prematurely gray hair and rather sharp features, but they were softened a bit by his horn-rimmed glasses and his marvelous warm smile. In his navy blue suit, he looked more like a teacher than a cab driver.

I wanted oysters to start, but Jerry said it was too late in the year to get good oysters, so I had littleneck clams and a red snapper with au gratin potatoes and for dessert the best pecan pie I've ever had in my life, served warm with thick whipped cream. It was perfect, and I decided that on Monday I would take my scale out and sell it, or throw it away; after all, I needed more space in the bathroom anyway.

"Jerry, forgive me for saying this, but you just don't seem like a cab driver. I mean, you're too classy and too nice and it just seems like you should be doing something much better. Why do you drive a taxi?"

"Freedom. Freedom. Barbara—and mobility. I work whenever I feel like working, and I can get around the city quickly and easily. I don't have to worry about finding a parking space. That's important to me because that's how I want to live, and also because I have a little business on the side—I guess Arnie told you about that."

"Yes. I'm not really into that."

"Not at all? Not even grass?"

"Oh, yeah, I like grass a lot, but it's not a big deal for me, you know? It's not a big part of my life."

"You've never had coke or speed?"

"No. And I'm not going to pretend I'm not curious or don't want to try them, but not now. I just started *my* own little business on the side, you know, and all at once there's been a rush of new experiences and new people for me. I've been through more new stuff in the past few months than in all the rest of my life, and I just need to slow it all down now so I can absorb it. Sometimes I feel like I'm on a jet plane going faster and faster, and I don't want it to go so fast that it flies right off the end of the earth."

"I understand. And I'd love to turn you on someday, but I'll be patient. What I've got planned for tonight may be a new experience for you, but I certainly hope that you'll go along with it."

I put my hand on Jerry's arm and smiled at him affectionately. "I'll probably go along with just about anything that doesn't involve needles or whips. I'm all ears."

"I thought we could go to Le Trapeze—my favorite night-club."

"Oh, that's that swing club, isn't it? Yes, I'd like that a lot. That's one new experience I do want—you'll find that I'm always willing to bend the rules, even when I make them."

"Great. I'm sure you'll like it. It's much better than Plato's Retreat—cleaner, plusher, and usually with much better people."

"I'd like to try Plato's sometime too, just because I've heard so much about it, and to see the difference for myself. Now we have a little matter to discuss, but I guess we'd better do that in the privacy of your cab."

Jerry smiled his agreement and paid the check and we drove down to Le Trapeze in his cab; he put the off-duty sign on and I sat next to him on the front seat. I asked him specifically what he had in mind, and he said he'd like to make it with me first and then we could swing with another couple; part of the turn-on, he said, was making love in the big orgy room and having people watch you while you watched them. Naturally, he said, I'd have the right of prior approval of the other couple; if the man didn't appeal to me, we'd just move on and find another couple. Saturday was a good night to go, Jerry said, because there was always a huge crowd. I suggested that we settle on the fee afterward, depending on what happened, and he said that was fine.

Trapeze was much nicer than I expected—very clubby and comfortable, and immaculate. It was very crowded, but that just made it seem more festive, and everyone was so friendly and sexy that there was no sense of crush. And all the nude bodies made it a feast for the eyes; almost all the men and women were young-looking and in good shape.

Straight ahead as you walked in was a counter for checking coats and a display case with fancy jock straps and panties for sale. On the right was a disco dance floor, and on the left a buffet with food and soft drinks and a small, cozy kind of living room where sex movies were shown continuously. The couples on the dance floor were mostly just dancing and those by the buffet were just eating and drinking, but the movie room was orgy time. One woman was on the carpet on her knees and elbows while a guy fucked her in the ass; both had their eyes fixed on the screen, where a skinny blonde was getting screwed in the cunt and the ass at the same time. At one end of the couch were two women and a man; one woman was sitting on the couch with her legs spread and the guy was next to her, facing the back with his knees on the couch, caressing her beautiful big tits and playing with her nipples; the other woman was on her knees in front of the couch, alternately eating out the woman and sucking the guy's asshole, and glancing up at the screen when she moved from one to the other. There was another threesome at the other end of the couch; a guy sat on the armrest, a woman knelt on the cushion and sucked him off slowly, while another guy fucked her from the rear. I felt it was a bit unfair that the woman didn't get to see the movie until I realized that there would probably be a rearrangement soon.

Jerry and I stood watching the scene for a minute, then looked at each other and grinned. We walked to the back through a wide hall with "private" rooms on either side;

these were cubicles with mattresses and doors. A few of the doors were open, and we could see foursomes carrying on as we walked by. In the back to the left was the orgy room, a big open space with wall-to-wall action. In the center was a big raised whirlpool bath, and to the right a locker room with showers and toilets. The attendant, a young guy in jeans and a T-shirt who seemed oblivious to all the beautiful breasts, legs, and asses around him, led us to a locker and handed us two clean towels. We got undressed, checking each other out and with a few strokes and caresses here and there; Jerry had a good body, skinny but muscular, and a nice big cock. We took our towels and were on our way.

"Can we try that whirlpool?" I said. "That looks very relaxing."

Jerry said I'd discover it was that and more, and we climbed in. The bath was deliciously warm and made you feel totally languorous and sensuous. I noticed that the most popular spots were the outlets where the jets of pulsing water came out. If you got right in front of the outlet and let the churning water hit you right between the legs or in your ass, you got a wonderfully erotic and intense kind of massage.

There was action all over this place; there had even been some nipple sucking and giving of head in the locker room, and more sucking and fucking went on around the whirlpool. There was a wonderful air of abandon and totally uninhibited sex that made Trapeze thrilling and exciting. But what really topped it all was the orgy room, where every kind of combination and freakout was going on at once. Jerry and I got out of the pool and toweled off and then went into the orgy room and just wandered around watching for a while. Then we found some empty mattress space and he pulled me down next to him.

We kissed and I licked his ears and neck and said, "Where do you want it?" and he said, "Everywhere." I sucked his armpits and his nipples and then moved down; he lifted himself up so I could suck his ass, and as I started I suddenly felt a tongue in my ass. I looked back and a guy with a black beard was grinning at me and saying, "Okay?" "Sure!" I said, and went back to sucking Jerry's ass while the bearded guy sucked my ass and my pussy. Jerry settled himself so I could suck his cock, then told me to sit on it. I climbed aboard Jerry and said, "Come here," to the bearded guy, taking his hand and standing him up next to me. I rode slowly up and down on Jerry and took the guy's hard-on in my mouth and sucked him, moving my tongue around the tip. Then I took my mouth off him and said, "Turn around," and he bent over so I could suck his ass. Jerry watched me, his face a mask of lust, and started to move frantically under me and then came in great spurts. I turned the other guy around and stroked his balls while I sucked him off lovingly, still sitting with Jerry inside me. The bearded guy put his hands gently behind my head and rocked back and forth, fucking me in the mouth, and came in a great hot load. "Swallow it," he said hoarsely, and I put my hands on his ass and drew him even closer and swallowed down his come. I could feel Jerry's eyes on me and other eyes on me and I took my mouth off the guy's cock very slowly and started cleaning it with my tongue, licking up and down and around the tip and sticking my tongue gently in his hole. I moved my hand back to his asshole and started stroking it with a finger. "Ummm—stick it in," he said, and I pushed my finger gently in and out of his asshole, still licking his cock. He stroked the back of my neck tenderly. I glanced down and saw a lovely tanned black-haired woman with full firm tits staring at me, her face bright with excitement. She was sitting by Jerry, and he reached over to fondle her pussy. She spread her legs to let him in and reached over to play with his nipples, then got up and lowered her ass over his face. He ate her wildly, then slowly, and she moaned and smiled at me and moved her tongue around her lips. I gave the bearded guy's cock a last kiss and climbed off Jerry; the brunette pulled me to her and kissed me, moving her tongue around inside my mouth. I squeezed her wonderful big tits and rubbed her nipples between my thumb and finger. Her nipples were big and as hard as a cock, and I couldn't stand it any longer; I took my mouth away from hers and sucked her nipples, going from one to the other hungrily, licking and sucking, while Jerry ate her out. He was hard again, and his cock was throbbing. She eased me down on the floor and got off Jerry and sucked my tits and then my pussy while Jerry fucked her from behind. She gave wonderful head, sucking Jerry's come out of me and rolling her tongue around my hole and sucking and licking my clit. So sweet, so tender, so wonderful. Jerry and I smiled at each other, and just as I started coming I could see him start to thrust harder and harder and come himself.

The woman and Jerry kind of collapsed on either side of me. The brunette took a minute or two to get herself together and then kissed Jerry and me and said she hoped she'd see us again. "Do you come here a lot?" I asked.

"Yes. My name is Danielle."

"I'm Barbara, and this is Jerry, and we're going to be coming here often."

Jerry laughed and said, "Okay! We'll be looking forward to seeing you," and she gave us a sexy little wave and walked away.

I looked at Jerry and said, "Wow. Beyond my wildest dreams. Are you ready for more? I don't think I can take much more tonight, but if you want—"

"Oh, no, are you kidding? I'm through for the night. Our other couple can wait till next time."

Jerry offered me a ride home, but I explained to him about wanting to keep my address secret and said if he could drop me off at Seventy-second and Third that would be fine.

He asked me how much I wanted.

"You know, this was so great, so warm and loving and sexy and frantic, it almost doesn't seem right to get paid for it. Especially if you're going to take me there often. So whatever you think—whatever you want to give me."

"It's not always quite as great as it was tonight—it all depends on who you meet. But it's always a lot of fun. And of course, I do want to take you there a lot. How about an even hundred, and then next time we can settle beforehand on whatever you want?"

"That's fine."

Jerry paid me and dropped me off and I promised to call him soon. I walked home in kind of a trance. For pure, wonderful, frantic sex, this had been the best night I'd ever had. Not love, but a lot of genuine warmth—and great, great sex. And my first woman; I had just been on the passive end, but I was ready for more; it would probably be easier at first with someone I didn't know too well. I started to fantasize about it and then I thought, *My, my, how kinky and wild you have become, Barbara, and so quickly.*

Little did I know. It was just the beginning.

IV. Unnatural Acts

I had launched myself into a new kind of sex life filled with acts that I once would have felt were much too kinky for me, even perverse—or *preverse,* as we used to say up dere in da Bronx—but that now I found pleasurable and often incredibly exciting.

One of the most popular things with all my customers is rimming, or licking and sucking the guy's ass. All those guys go absolutely wild over it, and I've gotten very good at it— lots of practice! The secrets are to do it for a long time— getting rimmed for just a few seconds is like eating only one peanut—and to vary the action every few minutes or so: sometimes licking gently and sometimes hard, or sucking, or rolling your tongue around and then sticking it in, really deep and slow one time and the next time in hard, fast jabs. But probably the best way for a sustained period of time is just to lick, back and forth and side to side, real slowly.

My clients almost always ask for this, not only because it feels so great but also because it's not something they usually want to ask their wives or girl friends for. And I know how they feel, because even though I absolutely delight in having it done to me, I had never once asked any of my lovers to do it. It wasn't until after I became a part-time call girl that I started asking my boyfriends to rim me, and that was part of generally becoming more willing and able to ask for what I wanted in sex. Before I became a part-timer, I was mostly passive in bed; I'd make a few hints now and then, by saying something or just moving to a certain position, but basically I let the guy lead the way.

And none of my lovers had ever asked me to do it for them. I did it for only one guy, a gorgeous hunk named Derek I met while I was still living at home and was crazy about. I never even knew it existed until he did it for me. One night he had been sucking my pussy and after a while he pulled his head away and rolled me over gently. I was so naïve then that I thought he just wanted to fuck me from behind, and I gasped when he stuck his tongue between the cheeks of my ass. That first time was the sweetest and most intense of all. I was moaning like mad, and I think that inspired Derek to do it really deeply and for a long time. The next time we had sex, I got carried away while I was sucking his cock and began stroking his asshole with my fingertip, then started licking it. After that it became a pretty regular part of our lovemaking. Good old Derek; he ended up marrying another girl from the Bronx. I've often been tempted to look him up and see what's happening with him, but I'm too afraid I'd have another fling with him and maybe break up his happy home.

Arnie is especially turned on by rimming, and we had a long talk about it one night after we'd finished a very hot session.

"It's one of those ultimate experiences," he said. "It's one of the most sensual things life has to offer—maybe *the* best."

"Oh, come on, Arnie. It's not *the* best. It's not as good as sex itself—I mean, it's not as good as coming."

"Well, it lasts longer. I mean, it can last longer. It's not as intense as an orgasm, but it can be almost so, and it's not over in a few seconds."

"Well, I don't agree, but I guess that's because women can come for a long time and men can't."

"That's true. I hadn't thought of it that way. But compare it to a great meal—that can be a pleasure almost as intense as sex, and it lasts for quite a long time, and there's a wider range of sensations—one different wonderful taste after another."

"Well, you're right, I guess, but this seems to me an awfully academic discussion, because you don't have to choose between these things—you can have all of them."

"Sometimes. But not everyone *wants* to come right out and ask for all of them."

"I know exactly what you mean. They would love it, but they're hesitant to ask for it, and even hesitant to do it. I don't quite understand why that is."

"You were never like that?"

"I was—that's just it. And I got it once or twice, and did it once or twice, but still I was shy about asking for it and didn't do it unless I was especially turned on. But that was because then I was passive sexually and let the guy lead the way. And I think one reason you guys are so crazy about it is that you won't ask a real lover to do it—right?"

Arnie leaned back on the pillow and gave a great sigh. "You know what it is? It's part of what they call the madonna-whore syndrome. It's the way American men are brought up. We divide all women into two kinds—the madonna or the nice girl, the sister or neighbor or wife or girl friend, the women we're supposed to put on a pedestal and idolize and take care of. And then there are the others—the whores—not necessarily real whores or semipros, but the sexually free and available women. It's a hangup for us, and a stupid one, but it's drummed into our heads all our lives— you can't come on to 'respectable' women, nice women, in a purely sexual way. You have to repress your desires until you prove your love or sincerity. It's that constant feminine refrain, 'I can't sleep with you unless you show me you really care about me and don't want me just for sex.' It reminds me of that old saying that men are led to love through sex and women are led to sex through love—that defines the madonna exactly. But I guess the whore type is like a man in this way—she can enjoy sex just for itself, and she can be led to love through sex, not the other way around."

"But that's not really true. I mean, we're all a mixture of the madonna and the whore—or rather we're really *neither*. We're just—women, you know. It depends on the guy, and how we feel, and a lot of other things."

"Well, no—it may be an oversimplification, like a lot of these schemes are, but there are some women who are open and free about sex and there are also a hell of a lot who use it as a way to manipulate men—maybe without even consciously intending to, but they do. But now, you know, I think I've lost track of what this has to do with our subject."

I laughed. "Ah, yes, let's get back to that. I think the connection is clear—it has to do with not being open and free and full of abandon. And I think that is *part* of it. But I think it's also because you feel that rimming is unnatural or kinky or weird or dirty—at least until you actually try it and realize it's not. I like to do it now—it gives me a warm feeling. I like to please, and this is pleasing someone in a very intimate and intense way. And everyone's clean—if someone wasn't clean, you wouldn't want to be with them in the first place."

Arnie nodded. "Right. And it's very erotic—but part of the reason it's so erotic is that it does have this air of the forbidden. That's the irony—we talk about being open and free and all that, but if these things didn't have this aspect of being secret, hidden, *taboo* desires, then maybe they wouldn't be as exciting."

"You know, maybe it's not a good idea to get into these things too deeply." I realized what I had said and burst out laughing. "No pun intended! But I mean, I love to do it and I love for guys to do it to me, and that's enough." It was getting very late, and I told Arnie I had to be going and got dressed and kissed him goodnight and headed for home.

But I was thinking in the cab about what he had said; *would* those things be so deliciously exciting if they weren't cloaked in this aura of secret sin? Would onions cost as much as truffles if onions were scarce? I decided that this was enough deep thinking for one night, and when I came out of it I suddenly noticed that the cab driver was a terrifically cute young guy. A rush of mischief came over me and I asked him, "Do you like onions?"

He looked at me in the rearview mirror and grinned. "Love 'em! Fried, smothered, raw with tomatoes—any way. You want to fix me some when we get you home?"

I laughed at his brashness, but I had to admit it was a great line. "I don't *usually* invite strange men up to my apartment."

"It means the ride is free."

"Oh, big deal! My culinary skills aren't for sale that cheap."

"You're absolutely right. Terribly ungentlemanly of me. Let me treat you at a restaurant."

I looked at the license on the dashboard; he even looked great in his mug shot, and his name was Joe Costiglio. "I'll tell you what, Joe. Give me your telephone number, and I may take you up on it some time."

"It's a deal!" he said, grabbing a sheet of paper from the seat next to him and handing it back to me. It was a kind of resumé, with telephone numbers for his home and his answering service on the top along with his description—five foot eleven, 155 pounds, black hair, olive eyes—and a listing of acting credits, for off-Broadway, off-off-Broadway and regional theater.

"Aha! You're an actor."

"Right! I just drive this to pay for my luxuries—like rent and onions."

We were pulling up to my building. "I'll call you," I said. "But there's just one problem."

"What's that?" Joe said, sounding not at all worried.

I handed him six dollars for the $4.20 fare and said, "You guys think about only one thing—food!" and got out. He laughed so hard he couldn't say anything and drove away with a wave.

My, my, Barbara, I thought to myself, *how* easy *you are. What a pushover.*

But not for everything. I may have been a quick pickup, and it had been very easy for me to get into rimming, but it was much harder to start on getting fucked in the ass. Now, I love it if I'm in the right mood and it's done right, but at first I was very reluctant, mainly because I thought it would hurt—but also because I didn't have any idea how much pleasure there could be in it. There were basically three things that finally got me started: constant requests from my customers, being rimmed as preparation by guys who were asking for it, and one of those far-out evenings on the town with Jerry the taxi driver.

I had called Jerry one Wednesday and asked him if he wanted to see me on Friday. Since he was always taking me to some wild place or trying to turn me on to some kind of what he jokingly called "controlled substances," I tried to limit dates with him to nights when I could sleep late the next day.

"Friday is great, Barbara. And I'm going to take you to a place that may shock you but that I think you'll like."

"Shock me! If it could shock me after Le Trapeze, it must be way too far out for me. What is it, Jerry—Madame Monique's Dungeon of a Thousand Tortures?"

He gave a lascivious chuckle and said, "That's not it, but if that's the kind of place you really want to go to, Barbara, I'm willing to accommodate your secret desires."

I laughed. "Wait till you see how hard I whip you—you may change your mind. But now stop teasing me and satisfy my curiosity—what is it?"

"It's a disco—a gay disco. But there are no real heavy scenes, and it's actually a lot of fun."

"By our standards it sounds very innocent. We can just

94

dance! But are women welcome there—or should I dress up in reverse drag in my tomboy outfit?"

"You're sure to get hit on if you do that. Wear your bikini —it's summertime and that'll help you keep your cool."

"That's a fine idea, but then where are you going to take me to dinner? Lutéce or The Four Seasons?"

Jerry chuckled again. "Barbara, you're a smartass. I'm going to call your bluff! Meet me at The Four Seasons at six, and wear your string bikini under whatever you want. You can strip down at the disco and I can watch you convert three hundred gay guys to the straight life instantly. You know, if I wasn't such a sweet guy I'd feed you at the disco buffet."

"Arghh! Anything but that! I'll see you at The Four Seasons."

What a wonderful and crazy guy. Jerry had me doubly intrigued: another great restaurant that was new to me and the gay disco. I'd never even had more than a nodding acquaintance with any gay guys, and now there were going to be hundreds. And although I didn't fully admit it to myself, I felt that kind of challenge I guess a lot of women feel: I was going to convert one of those guys and show him what he'd been missing.

I left work a few minutes early—you can get away with that on a Friday—to change for our date, and I decided I'd take Jerry up on his dare. I didn't have a string bikini, but I didn't want to disappoint Jerry, so I had gone out and bought one on my lunch hour. I couldn't believe that so little cloth could cost so much money—forty-five bucks!—but I thought, what the hell, it would last for quite a while. The bottom was tiny, with barely enough material to cover my pussy and almost none at all to cover my ass, just literally a string up the back. The top was also tiny, and since I'm not used to wearing a bra anyway it hardly seemed worth bothering with the top. I wore my black cocktail dress with the slit skirt and a pair of heels, and I was off and running.

The Four Seasons is an incredible room—a ceiling that seems as high as the sky, great rippling curtains of what looks like gold chain, and acres and acres of space. Jerry was wearing his summer ice-cream suit with a white shirt and a pale yellow tie, and he looked cool in every sense of the word, and adorable. And he was in a great upbeat mood. I decided that if I was going to be throwing myself around dancing I needed to have a light meal, so I ordered Scotch salmon to start—a gigantic plate of that delicate but wondrously tasty stuff with its marvelously sensual texture—and we shared a striped bass with fennel and fresh raspberries.

I told Jerry that I couldn't help but be curious about what the attraction of a gay disco was for him, and he said it was mainly that it was even wilder and less inhibited than an ordinary disco—you could dance in just a jock strap if you felt like it. I asked him if he had ever been tempted by any of the guys, and he said, "Occasionally, I must admit. I don't think I'd really mind fucking one of those guys, or getting rimmed and blown, but I've never taken advantage of any of my numerous opportunities. I've never been quite able to bring myself to actually do it—I guess I'm afraid of what it might lead to. I might discover I'm really bisexual. Of course they say the great advantage of being bi is that it doubles your chances of getting a date for Saturday night, but I don't know whether I'm really ready for it yet. Maybe some day."

"Well, if it bothers you, why not just go to an ordinary disco? You can let yourself go almost as much at one of those, can't you? The difference isn't that much."

"Barbara, I may as well admit the truth, because *you'll* discover it anyway. The real reason I go there is that those guys are great customers."

"Aha! The real shame comes out. It's all business. What do they like mainly? It's not smack, is it?"

"No, none of them will touch that. It kills your sexual desire. But they all love coke and speed and especially poppers."

"Poppers? What's that?"

"Amyl nitrate. You snort it before you come, and it gives you an incredibly intense orgasm."

"Wow. Now that sounds like a good drug. Have you ever tried it?"

"Only once. It works, but it also made me feel as if I were going to have a heart attack. Too scary to make it worthwhile."

"Enough said. I'll take your word for it, and I'll pass. Well, one more cup of espresso and then I'm ready whenever you are."

"Anytime. Now tell me—what are you wearing, if anything, under that sexy dress?"

I grinned at him. "The bottom half of the tiniest, teensiest, weeniest string bikini you've ever seen. You may not be able to control yourself. Even *they* may not, when they see the ass. But are you sure I'm not going to feel unwelcome?"

"Oh, no. There's always at least half a dozen women there. Just be cool and don't come on the wrong way, and they'll love you. It's a very live-and-let-live kind of atmosphere, believe me."

The disco was on the West Side in that kind of never-never land between Chelsea and the Village, and even though it was just after eight o'clock the place was already crowded. At first it seemed like any other disco—blaring music and flashing lights and dancing. But then you noticed that it was just as Jerry had said—the dancing was much wilder, and the population was ninety-nine percent male, and a lot of the guys were wearing just shorts or jock straps. Almost all of them had great-looking bodies. I saw just a few women, dancing with great abandon all by themselves; most were wearing shorts and halters but one beautiful black chick with big firm tits had on just a pair of panties. No one, not surprisingly, was paying any attention to the women.

"Let's get comfortable," Jerry said. He took off everything except his shorts, and I stripped down to my panties and we stashed everything at the checkroom. We just walked around for a while looking at the scene, and then started to dance. It really was different—the intense air of freedom and abandon got to you, and it felt wonderful to dance almost nude. You could forget all your cares and lose yourself totally in the dancing and the music. Finally we both reached the point of exhaustion and headed for the bar to rest up and take a little liquid stimulation.

In my innocence I ordered Delamain, and the bartender, a handsome black-haired guy in a T-shirt and shorts, smiled and said gently, "Sorry—the only brandy we have is Martell," so I settled for that.

"No fancy drinks here," Jerry said. "Just your basic strong stuff. The point is to take care of the head, not the palate."

"But this is fun!" I said. "This was a great idea."

"There's more. There's a very interesting back room, if you're in a kinky mood."

I took his arm and said, "Jerry, when I'm with you, I'm always in a kinky mood," and we walked back there. I guessed on the way what it was, and of course I turned out to be right—it was an orgy room. There was just no way those guys could work up all that sexual energy on the dance floor and then wait until they got home to work it off.

The scene in the back room made Le Trapeze look like a nunnery. There were threesomes and foursomes and even a few twosomes, and several people like Jerry and me just enjoying the show, including that lovely bare-breasted black girl I had seen earlier. One guy was fucking another in the ass; the guy getting screwed was sucking someone's cock, and a fourth man was sucking the ass of the guy doing the fucking. There were several threesomes with men getting rimmed and blown at the same time, and three groups where a guy was screwing someone in the ass while getting fucked himself.

I glanced over at Jerry, who had a huge hard-on, and I

sensed that it was probably only a matter of time before he got into this scene, at least as an active if not passive participant. He had kept his shorts on, and I guess they were a symbol of his separation from what was going on around him, a kind of armor that protected him from desires he didn't want to let himself act on. I felt that I could put his mind at rest for the moment by being his woman, so I moved closer to him and started stroking his hard-on through his shorts. I hadn't really planned for us to make it there, but I thought, *Why not?* The time and the place were just right and we were already undressed.

Jerry put an arm around me and started caressing my breast. Then he noticed someone he knew and murmured, "Oh, there's Eric," and led me a few feet farther back so we could say hello to Eric. It turned out that Eric was one of the men in the middle, screwing and getting screwed at the same time. "Hello, Pierre!" Jerry yelled, and got a wolfish grin and a "Hi, Jerry!" in return.

"Pierre?" I said. "I thought his name was Eric."

Jerry smiled at me patiently and explained. "It's from an old joke that isn't really very funny but has a classic punch line. An old Frenchwoman, a concierge, spies every night on the three homosexuals across the way. One evening she has a friend over, another elderly lady, and unfortunately there's no action to be seen that night, so the concierge tells her friend about the great show that's usually presented. 'Sometimes it's just two, you know, but often all three get together and Pierre screws Jean while Jacques screws Pierre.' 'Ah,' her friend says with a sigh. 'Lucky Pierre—always in the middle.'"

I giggled; it was cute. We watched Eric finish his threesome with a look of intense pleasure on his face; apparently he was coming as the other guy was coming in him. Then Eric bade his friends or acquaintances or whoever they were farewell and came over to greet us. He looked to be about twenty and was a bit skinny but very muscular and good-looking, with blond hair and perfect features; from the neck up, at least, he looked like a model. He shook hands with Jerry and gave me a sweet smile as Jerry introduced us; I managed a pleasant "How are you?" but it felt funny to be standing there almost naked in front of a nude guy I had just been watching in this wild sex scene—especially funny because he didn't look at my body or register any interest. But he seemed very nice and pleasant and at ease, so that helped put me at ease.

"Do you want to stay longer," Jerry asked him, "or should we all go out for a drink or a bite to eat?"

Eric laughed. "God, no—I've had it for tonight and I'm ready to leave. Just give me a minute to take a quick shower and get dressed."

"Great," Jerry said. "We'll put our clothes on and meet you by the checkroom."

When we got to the checkroom, the beautiful black girl was standing at the counter getting her clothes—a white blouse and shorts. She glanced at me and smiled warmly and said, "How did you like it?"

I laughed. "I guess you could tell it was my first time here. It was fun—and certainly different. Do you come here a lot?"

"Oh, yeah. I come with a gay friend. I love it just for the dancing—I can dance my head off here without worrying about eighty guys trying to hit on me."

Jerry was watching her intently as she put her clothes on. "Haven't I seen you in Plato's?" he asked.

She gave a delightful laugh. "I'm sure you have. That's my other bag. My name is Lillian, and I guess I'll see you two at Plato's sometime?"

"I certainly hope so. I'm Jerry, and this is Barbara."

"Nice to meet you—and we'll run into you soon. Have fun!"

Eric came up and met us and said, "I'm starved. I could really go for a steak at the Lion's Head—or wherever you want. Of course," he went on, giving me a big wink, "if I know Jerry, you've probably already had a gigantic dinner at Lutèce or Twenty-One."

"Twenty-One!" Jerry exclaimed with great indignation. "I don't eat that garbage! Someday, Eric, I'm going to educate your palate. And if you must know, it was The Four Seasons. Now how about Maxwell's Plum? It's better steak than the Lion's Head, and Barbara and I can have something light. And besides, maybe you can pick up a girl."

"Maxwell's is fine, but you have to stop trying to convert me. By the time that happens, I'll have converted *you*"—and another mischievous wink for me. I could see that I was going to like Eric a lot.

We went outside and got into Jerry's cab—all three of us in the front seat so Jerry didn't feel like he was working—and headed uptown. Eric asked me if I had enjoyed myself and I said yes, then couldn't stop myself from adding, "And you sure looked like you were having a great time."

Eric laughed. "Ah, yes, yes. Sometimes a quiet little evening at home, and sometimes a nice flashy flameout in public. I guess I truly am an exhibitionist at heart."

"But doesn't it—I guess I shouldn't really ask you this—"

"Oh," Jerry interrupted, "you can ask him anything you want. He's the world's leading expert on depraved sexuality. Just don't ask him about sensitive personal subjects like making a living."

"Oh, fuck you," Eric said, and Jerry muttered, "You'd love it." Eric ignored him and said to me, "Please, go ahead. It's impossible to embarrass me. You mean, doesn't it bother me to have people watching?"

"Oh, no, I can understand that—that just makes it more exciting. But I mean, doesn't it *hurt*—to do that?"

"Oh, no, not if you do it right. If the cock goes in very slowly at first, if the guy doesn't try to jam it all in at once, it's fine. And once it's in, it feels fantastic. It hits the prostate, you know, massages the prostate, and that feels wonderful and practically makes you come just that way."

"Oh, Lord, Lord," Jerry said, "do we have to get so goddamn *clinical?*"

"Just drive," Eric said, "and try to keep your excitement under control."

And I said, "No, no, go on—I'm getting myself an *education* here."

"Well, that's basically it," Eric said. "And of course when you take the active role, it feels tremendous because it's so tight and hot. Now if I can ask you a personal question, have you ever—"

"No, not yet—I've been wanting to try it but I've been afraid because I thought it would hurt. But if you say it—well, I must admit I'm getting curiouser and curiouser. And speaking of curious, and since we're being so open with each other, have you ever been with a woman?"

"Forget it, Barbara," Jerry said. "It's hopeless, just hopeless."

"He's right," Eric said. "No curiosity there—no desire. I'm very happy the way I am. That old line about 'Show me a happy homosexual, and I'll show you a corpse'—that's just antigay bullshit."

"Thank God we're here!" Jerry said. "Now we can start talking about food."

"Where did you meet *him?*" Eric said to me. He was the first gay guy I had ever really talked to, but he had my kind of sense of humor, and I liked him more and more as the evening went on.

It was after eleven, and the back room at Maxwell's Plum was supposed to be closed, but all three of us liked it much better than the café part in front because it's more plush and roomy and comfortable. Jerry knows the captains in the back room, and since the room was still crowded and going full blast we decided to give it a try. Jerry is a very good tipper, and when he asked the maître d'hotel, "Are we too late to be seated back here?" the reply was a big smile and a handshake and "For you, Mr. Jenkins, it's never too late."

Eric was indeed starved and ordered black bean soup and a spinach salad and a steak with french fries, but Jerry and I just wanted something light. "You know," I said, "what I'd love is eggs benedict, but I don't think they make them in the evening."

"Great idea," Jerry said, "that sounds perfect." He asked the captain, "Do you think you could talk the chef into making two orders of eggs benedict?"

"Absolutely, Mr. Jenkins. And would—"

"Oh, look at those balloons!" Eric was all excited. He had looked up at the cut-glass ceiling in the back room, with its beautiful patterns of colors, and nestled up against it were the balloons, with swirling designs in lighter and brighter colors, that diners had released to float upward. "Can we have balloons too?"

"Of course, sir," the captain said with great solemnity, as if Eric had asked for extra tarragon in his bearnaise sauce. "How many would you like?"

"Four!" said Eric, like a little kid at a birthday party. "One each for the lady and the gentleman, and *two* for me."

I giggled. "Eric, you're too much. Now tell me the story of your life. I guess you have a big inheritance?"

The captain brought the balloons and tied all four of them to the back of Eric's chair. Eric stroked them and bounced them about with delight and grinned at me. "Inheritance! I wish! I'm a kept boy; a very sweet and very rich young man from Morristown, New Jersey, takes care of all my needs. Well, most of my needs. And occasionally I sell my beautiful body to some very wealthy men."

"Eric," Jerry said darkly, "is a part-time hooker."

"Oh, my," I said. "Oh, my."

"Oh, don't be shocked, Barbara. It's all done very elegantly. And as I say, these are *really* rich men. The only

103

reason I hang out with a poor slob like Jerry is that he brings me good things for the head. And he does know the fine restaurants."

That last remark was all Jerry needed, and we spent the rest of the meal talking about food. That is, Jerry and I did —Eric mostly ate and listened. But I very much wanted to get to know Eric better and thought he would make a wonderful friend for me—someone I could confide everything to and a male friend who wouldn't complicate my already too-complicated emotional life. So when dessert time came— Jerry and I shared one order of strawberries and Eric had a huge piece of chocolate cake—I said, "Eric, can I call you sometime? Maybe we can get together for dinner or whatever."

He gave me a frank, affectionate look and said, "I'd like that. Here's my number; I live in the Village. But please don't call before noon."

We sat there for another half-hour drinking espresso and smoking and discussing some further entertainment; it turned out that Eric was a fellow jazz fan. But we finally decided to just wrap things up with Eric and Jerry transacting their business at Jerry's apartment in SoHo, and then Jerry and I would be all set either to stay there or go to one of the swing clubs. So we piled back into the cab; Jerry took the East River Drive, and in ten minutes we were at his apartment, a big loft with an elaborate stereo and video system and a bedroom with a huge double bed and a mirror on the ceiling. Jerry poured us all a little cognac, then gave Eric an innocent-looking manila envelope for which Eric forked over three hundred-dollar bills.

"What is that?" I asked. "I guess if it costs that much, it must be coke."

"You guessed it," Jerry said. "And I think tonight is gonna be the night I turn you on to some of this really topnotch stuff."

Eric gave me another big wink and said, "Make sure he

takes good care of you. If he doesn't, I want to hear about it." He gave me a hug and a kiss and said goodnight to us; Jerry offered him a ride home, but Eric said he was going to drop in on a friend nearby.

I had had lots of food and wine and espresso already, and now the cognac, so I was a little hesitant to try the coke on top of all that, but I was intensely curious to see what it was like. I was even more curious to see what it was like to get fucked in the ass, and I sensed that Jerry wanted tonight to be the time for that. I thought that maybe the coke would help loosen me up for the ass fucking.

"Do you want to stay here," Jerry asked, "or should we go to Plato's or Le Trapeze?"

"Oh, let's not go out again—we're here, we're comfortable, and we can get really comfortable. We can go to a swing club anytime. And besides, Jerry, I'm all ready to offer you my last piece of virginity, and I'd just as soon do that in private. But if you've got your heart set on a club, then of course I'll be happy to go."

"Oh, no, I'm with you. Let's go in the bedroom and get comfortable and I can offer you a little snort."

I sat down on that big bed. There was easily room for four, and I asked Jerry if there had ever been that many. "Three has been the most so far, but that's a great idea."

I took off my clothes, looking at myself in the mirror on the ceiling and starting to feel very sexy. There is something very erotic about watching yourself in the mirror, and I played with my nipples and my pussy, looking at the reflection and being the exhibitionist and the voyeur all at the same time.

Jerry had taken his clothes off and was standing at the night table with a big hard-on, trying to line out the coke and watch me at the same time. "You're making it hard to concentrate," he said.

I laughed. "I'm sorry—I'll stop. But I was really getting into admiring myself. Now just give me a little bit, please—

remember this is my first time. And tell me what it's like. How does it make you feel?"

"You'll get a wonderful rush—it feels like having an orgasm all over your body. And it intensifies everything, all your sensations. It's a terrific high—by far the best there is."

He scraped what looked to me like an awful lot of coke onto a card and sat down next to me on the bed, giving me a deep French kiss, as if for encouragement. I stroked his hard cock while he held the card up to my nose. "Just snort it up fast and hard, then lie back and give it a few minutes and wait for heaven to open up for you."

I snorted three or four times; it felt kind of cold and ticklish, but nice. I lay back on the bed and Jerry put some coke on the card for himself and snorted it, then put the card down and started sucking my nipples. That felt sweet and delicious like it always does, but then I felt a glow and a kind of chill at the same time, and it seemed as if he was sucking all over my body at once, and my nipples got harder and harder and seemed to almost vibrate with an intense thrill of pleasure. I looked up at the mirror and everything seemed sharper and brighter, with deeper colors and incredibly sharp outlines. It was like when you put on someone else's glasses and the world jumps into a sharper focus, but there was also a bright clear light, an almost blinding shine on everything, like looking into the sun. A surge of energy went through my body, and I spread my legs wide and started writhing on the bed; I could feel my heart beating very fast, and I got lightheaded from the rush and the intensity and the brightness.

Jerry moved his head down and started licking my clit, and I jumped and gasped as if a jolt of electricity had gone through me. "Wow, oh, wow," I moaned, but the sound of my voice seemed deafeningly loud, like a stereo turned up full blast, and it echoed around the room. The more I moaned, the more amplified it seemed. I started coming with great shudders and came and came for what seemed like an hour. I watched myself writhe in the mirror and listened to myself moaning but even as the sounds and the images got more and more intense, they seemed to drop away into another world and I was all just inside myself, inside my cunt, coming and coming convulsively like I never had before.

Finally Jerry pulled his head away and lay next to me and kissed me deeply; I moved my tongue all over his mouth and the taste of myself seemed to explode on my palate, like sweet grapes bursting with juice under your tongue. When we stopped, I looked down at his cock; it was huge and hard and seemed to fill my whole field of vision. I went after it with my tongue, licking it with quick jabbing strokes, then licking it up and down, running my tongue around the tip, then going to suck his balls and his asshole, and coming back to lick and suck his cock, going two hundred miles an hour. Jerry was getting too hot and too close to coming; he told me to put my head down and my ass up in the air by the edge of the bed.

From far away somewhere I heard myself saying, "Do it, do it, but have you got something to get me ready, some Vaseline or something?" Jerry said, "I've got much better than that," and stuck his tongue in my asshole and started licking like mad. He did it for what seemed like hours, licking and sucking, and then he jabbed his tongue in, first a little way and then deeper and deeper, like a miniature cock. I moaned with wave after wave of pleasure and felt myself drifting out of the world again into a kind of trance where the only thing that existed was the sweetness and joy of this incredible delight. Jerry had been absolutely right; this was the best way to make me really want to take him up my ass.

Finally I needed more, I wanted the completion of it, and I said, "Jerry, stick your cock in, fuck me in the ass." He sucked me for another minute, then stood up and gently put a finger in just a little bit, to loosen me up more. He pulled his finger out slowly and put his cock on my asshole and very slowly, very gently pushed just the tip in. He stayed there a moment, then pushed in another inch or so, and I felt a quick twinge of pain but then a wonderful fullness and tightness. "Okay?" he said. "Yes, yes!—stick it all in, fuck me in the ass." He plunged all the way in, and it was an incredibly erotic, exciting sensation. A great feeling of joyous submissiveness and abandon came over me, and I wanted to be his whore and do anything he asked.

"Am I tight enough, Jerry? Am I good for you? Fuck me harder." I could feel myself gripping his cock ever so tightly and I tried to contract my ass so he would feel me even more. I couldn't quite do it the first few times I tried, but then I got the hang of it and did it over and over and he said, "Oh, God, God, that feels great, that feels so great." He started thrusting faster and faster, and I could feel the very first beginnings of him starting to come and then felt him exploding inside me and his hot come in my ass. "Oh, I can *feel* you coming!" I yelled, and in that way it was much more intense than getting fucked in the cunt, a completely different kind of pleasure. Jerry pulled out slowly, and that was the final tantalizing sensation to top it all off—or bottom it all off, I should say!

We both collapsed on the bed. The coke rush had worn off, and I felt totally, excruciatingly exhausted. I put my arm around Jerry and snuggled my head by his shoulder, and the next thing I remember is waking up and seeing the faint light of the dawn through the Venetian blinds and then falling back to sleep again.

I woke up for good at about one o'clock; the sun was streaming into the room, and I felt refreshed and renewed but very lazy. Jerry had gone and I had that whole huge bed all to myself. I just lay there for a while, enjoying the feeling and savoring the luxury of not having to get up. It struck me that although I never wanted to go full-time, the chance to sleep late every day, to *never again* get up with the alarm, would certainly be the biggest temptation to become a real call girl. I stretched luxuriously, and suddenly I got an inspiration: I hadn't had breakfast in bed for a long time. But I had no idea where Jerry was, or even if he was still in the apartment. Just then, I heard him moving around in the living room, being quiet so he wouldn't wake me, and I called his name.

He came in and beamed at me. "Good morning, beautiful. How do you feel?"

"Great. Ten hours of sleep can fix me up from anything. But you know what would make it all just perfect?"

Jerry burst out laughing. "Barbara, you're *insatiable*. And first thing in the morning!"

"No, no, not that, you horny bastard. First thing in the morning is a horrible time for that—for love or money. Even both. No, I was just thinking that I haven't had breakfast in bed for years, and right now seems like the perfect time."

"Good idea. You got it—anything you want. But I must tell you that I make the best scrambled eggs in the world. Orange or grapefruit juice, take your pick. Freshly squeezed, of course. Bacon if you want. Whole-wheat bread from Zito's for toast. And of course espresso."

"That sounds wonderful—but too much. Just like the coke—wonderful, but I think a little too much. Grapefruit juice, and we'll have to see if your scrambled eggs are really as good as you say, and one *small* slice of toast, please, and no bacon. I've got to try to preserve what's left of my figure."

"Coming right up. And a big pot of espresso—with a regular cup, not a demitasse."

I smiled at him warmly. "Jerry, you're marvelous. Will you marry me?"

"What! And be stuck in the kitchen all day, slaving away behind a hot stove? No way. I'd say no even if you were serious—I need my freedom. Jam or honey for your toast?"

"Just butter. I'm too sweet already."

Jerry was back in a few minutes with a tray. The juice was

fabulous, sweet and tart and cold and frothy, the toast grainy and crusty and hot, and the eggs just as terrific as Jerry had promised—incredibly creamy and voluptuously soft, with a gentle peppery heat that set off the richness perfectly.

"Wow. These are superb. What's your secret?"

"Cooking them very slowly, and an extra yolk—you use two eggs and then add just the yolk from a third egg. And then grind in a lot of fresh pepper before you beat them."

"They're fantastic. And last night was fantastic—I discovered Eric, and coke, and ass fucking."

Jerry smiled. "And now you're ready for more of all three."

"Ummm. I like Eric a lot. Does he know about us—I mean, about our arrangement."

"No, of course not. I would never tell anyone, and certainly not without your permission. But you'd be perfectly safe telling him. He is absolutely discreet when he needs to be, and you can trust him with anything. He's totally honest and real, and a very loyal friend. We tease each other a lot, as you heard, but we've been good friends for more than a year. He's very into coke, but he's not a cokehead—he's not addicted. He keeps it under control; I've seen him go a month without any of it. The only thing he doesn't keep under control is sex."

"I loved the coke, but like I said it was a little *too* intense. Could we try half that amount next time?"

"Sure. I really gave you very little, but it affects people differently. But don't you get hooked now—don't do it more than once a week, at the most."

"No, believe me, I wouldn't want to. I tend to overdose on things I like, food and espresso, and I know that, so that makes me want to be very careful, especially with all the horror stories I've heard about people fucking up their lives with snorting and shooting."

"And that leaves your third discovery, the Greek. Not

much danger in overdosing on that," Jerry said with a lascivious smile.

I laughed. "Jerry, you're a freak! No, it is wonderful, and I'm definitely going to do a lot more of it. But no overdosing, because I'm going to have to be in the right mood, and it's going to have to be with someone like you who's gentle and knows how to do it right. And all my guys ask for it, you know? I guess that's because they don't want to ask their wives or girl friends to do it."

Jerry shrugged. "Yeah—well, you know, you just feel more comfortable asking for it when you're paying and there's no emotional involvement—well, there is emotional involvement, but there's less at *stake*. You know." Jerry looked uncomfortable.

"That's all right. I know. But I wouldn't be turned off otherwise, and I think most women wouldn't, if the approach was right—gradual and gentle and not demanding—and there was the right preparation. Patience is the thing, but men aren't always patient."

"Well, it's not our nature to be patient in sex—it's male physiology. Like that old saying that a hard cock has no conscience—it has no patience either. But speaking of paying for things, let's settle up."

"My business adviser says Greek is a hundred fifty, so I guess I have to go along with that. But I had such a great time with you, like I always do, that I should be willing to negotiate. On the other hand, I broke a very strict rule of mine by doing an all-nighter."

"Oh, no, this wasn't an all-nighter, this was a sleepover—a bed and breakfast. But I don't want to negotiate or haggle—I want to give you the one fifty. Haggling isn't my style, as you may have noticed."

"I know—I shouldn't have even said that. And you're right—it wasn't really an all-nighter like I usually think of it; I could have left here last night, but God knows I wasn't in any shape to do so. Jerry, listen. It's not that I'm cold and unemotional, and it's not that I don't appreciate a fabulous evening like last night and a wonderful morning like this. It's just that if I didn't distance myself a little bit from this business, I'd go *crazy*. I can't let myself fall for my customers. Sometimes I wake up in the middle of the night and a little voice in my head says, 'You like these guys who pay you better than your *real lover*. You like these guys who pay you *better* than the man who really loves you.' Over and over. And I say to the voice, 'Shut up!' And I try to go back to sleep. But I can't, because I know it's at least partly true. But I don't know whether it's good or bad or what to do about it. And I don't like to think about it—I hate things like this buzzing around in my head all the time. This self-analysis bit just isn't my thing. It's just not *me*. I try to enjoy life and treat people right and make enough money so I don't have to worry all the time. And that's it. Ten years from now, when I get married and have a family, then maybe I'll get into these things deeper, the meaning of life and all that, but right now I don't want to live my life inside my head. You're only young once, right? If you don't enjoy your carefree youth when you're young, then when?"

Jerry looked at me very thoughtfully and nodded slowly. "I know what you mean. And I think you're right. You know, a doorman hailed me the other day on Fifth Avenue around Eighty-ninth Street. A guy gets in the cab and says, 'Sloan-Kettering.' Well, you know what that means. He looks to be about fifty, and he's got cancer. We start talking, and it turns out they've got him on a very strict diet and chemotherapy but they still give him only about a year to live. He says, 'With all my money, I can't even sit down and have a steak and a glass of beer.' And when he gets out of the cab at the hospital, he says to me, 'Try to remember one thing. The purpose of this life is to enjoy it.' "

"Yeah—that's it exactly. Jerry, I'm sorry—I didn't mean to cry on your shoulder and get us into a sad bag, but I just —well, you know, it feels better to get it off your chest."

"Absolutely. I'm glad you did. That's why I think Eric would be a great friend for you. In a lot of ways, women can get closer to a gay guy."

"I'm going to call him soon. And speaking of friends, I think I'd better get home before some of mine start wondering what's happened to me."

I finished my second cup of espresso and got dressed. Jerry paid me and we had a long affectionate good-bye kiss and I promised to call him soon.

I walked out into the bright sunlight and the Saturday crowds of SoHo. I felt a faint sense of unreality about it all—maybe having crammed too much into the last twenty-four hours or maybe some lingering aftereffects of the coke. But anyway I felt I needed to get home and touch base with myself literally and figuratively. When I walked into my apartment, I felt better immediately. I found messages on my answering machine from Kathy and Michael, and I decided that the rest of the weekend would be devoted to friends and my own personal life and that when I did see a customer again during the next week it should be a change of pace.

And the perfect change of pace, of course, was Mitch. But surprisingly enough, part of my education in the kinkier kinds of sex came from him—my most innocent customer. Or really from my teaching him. It made me think of that line from *The King and I*—"If you become a teacher, by your students you'll be taught." In the process of showing Mitch things and trying to teach him how to please a woman, I learned a lot about what really turns men on and how to help them pace themselves.

I called Mitch on Monday, and we set up a date for Wednesday evening. When I arrived at his apartment he had already gotten quite comfortable; he was wearing only a bath towel. And he was ready to go right to work. I sat down on the couch and said, "Mitch, let's take a few minutes to talk first. And could I have a glass of that sherry?"

"My God! I almost forgot! I have something special for you." He went into the kitchen and came back with a bottle of Delamain and a snifter.

"Great! How did you know that's my favorite? Oh, of course you heard from our mutual friend. But that's very sweet of you, Mitch. And you see why it's never a good idea to rush a woman? I would have missed both the cognac and knowing how considerate you were."

He nodded thoughtfully. "You're right. And Barbara, I do want you to teach me." He gave me that wonderful leer and added, "It will be the most fun I've had studying since Tax Code 101."

"It will be a blast. And you'll probably figure out a way to take my fees off your taxes. Now lesson one is, like I said, don't rush. Women don't like that. And don't be too anxious —that's a real turn-off. Act self-assured—even if you don't feel that way."

Mitch looked thoughtful again. "Right. Okay. And lesson two?"

I took another sip of cognac, stood up, and took his hand. "For lesson two we have to go into the bedroom. Come to think of it, lesson two may be the most valuable one of all. It's something that, would you believe it, many men don't know."

As I was getting undressed, Mitch said, "Now you've got me really intrigued—something a lot of men don't know?"

"Well, I shouldn't really say many men; I haven't been with that many. All I know is that many of the guys I have gone to bed with don't know it, and according to what I hear from my girl friends, a good unscientific guess is that certainly more than half of all men don't. Or maybe a lot of them do know but just don't like to do it."

"They don't like to do it? Is it unpleasant?"

I giggled. Mitch was so nice and innocent and such an

eager student! He not only brought out the maternal instinct but also made me feel like a sister or at least a very close friend.

"No, not at all—once you try it, you'll love it. All my other customers love to do it to me, and every *good* lover I've ever had—I mean nonpaying lover—has too. I guess maybe some guys *think* they wouldn't like it, but if they'd just experiment once, they'd probably end up being devoted to it—like learning to love snails or oysters." I giggled again; that somehow didn't seem like the best possible comparison.

A glimmer of understanding was dawning on Mitch's face. "Aha. You're being a real tease by piquing my curiosity and not satisfying it, but I think I'm beginning to get the idea."

I was lying on the bed and Mitch was sitting by my side; I spread my legs invitingly and reached up to stroke the back of his neck, then gently guided his head toward my pussy. He had indeed caught on to the idea, but not to the technique; he was sticking his tongue in and out of my cunt hard and fast and rough.

"No, Mitch, no," I said, and pulled away from him. "There are two words about pleasing a woman that you should always remember—no matter what you're doing in bed, they always apply. Slow and gentle. Slow and gentle. And don't start there, in the vagina; start on the clit." I wasn't sure whether he knew where it was or not, so I tried to choose my words carefully so I could guide him but he wouldn't feel insulted if he did know where it was. "Just move your tongue up and lick that sweet little bud, back and forth, slow and gently. That's it . . . ummm. Now straight up and down, not side to side . . . now just on the top of it, up and down . . . a little harder . . . perfect . . . now suck it with your lips . . . *gently* . . . wonderful . . . now suck it and roll your tongue around it at the same time . . . ummm . . . wow . . . do that for a while."

Mitch had turned out to be a very quick study, and I just

lay there for a while enjoying it and moaning softly. Then I had a brainstorm and realized I could offer him a perfect, vivid demonstration of why this kind of foreplay was so great and valuable.

"Okay—now put your tongue back in my cunt and just roll it around gently—around the sides mostly, and in and out a little bit. That's it. And do you notice any difference from before?"

Mitch lifted his head and gave me a big sexy smile. "Juicier and tastier!" And he smacked his lips with gusto like a true gourmet.

I laughed and reached out to ruffle his hair. "Mitch, lesson three was going to be on developing a sense of humor, but you've already mastered that. Give me a little more head, and we'll move on to the main event."

Mitch sucked me for a few more minutes, going back and forth from my clit to my cunt like a true expert, and I got carried away and started to come, urging him on and telling him that now was the time to go faster and concentrate on the clit. He did beautifully, and I felt a big rush of pride and tenderness for him. I wanted to start sucking his cock, but I was afraid he was so hot that he'd come too soon, like he had on our first date, so I told him to climb on top of me.

He did, but with all his weight, and he couldn't find my pussy to enter me. "Mitch, put your weight on your elbows, so you don't crush me. Right." I reached down and guided him home with my hand, and of course he immediately began thrusting frantically, quick and hard.

"Okay," I said patiently. "What are we doing wrong now? What are the two words that always apply?"

"Right. Right. Sorry." And he slowed down a little bit, but he was already too far along and when he started to come of course he went up to a hundred miles an hour again, and the whole thing was over in about half a minute.

He pulled out right away and gave me a kiss. "Wow," he

said apologetically, "I guess that's too fast, but it can't be too slow either—you know?"

"I know, and that's where *you* can teach *me*—how to help a man pace himself so he doesn't come too quickly and can last longer."

Mitch plopped himself down onto the bed, put his hands behind his head, and stared at the ceiling. "I don't know whether I really can. The best way is to have a lot of sex all the time—then it's easier to take your time and not come so fast, because that tremendous urgency isn't there. But you know, I have noticed one thing—when I masturbate, it's easier to slow down and make it last longer."

"That's because you're totally in control of what's happening and you can slow down or change what you're doing, right?"

"Exactly." He took his eyes off the ceiling and looked at me. "And I can guess what you're going to say now: that you can do the same things during actual sex. But that takes practice, I guess."

"Practice—and a good partner. I think a lot of this is actually up to the woman. She should know how to change the pace and switch from one thing to another—like when she's sucking the guy's cock, she can stop for a while and suck his balls or just lick his cock or—or whatever." I had been all ready to say "or suck his ass," but I realized just in time that I had never rimmed Mitch and that such an advanced subject should probably wait until our next lesson. I didn't want to throw too much at him all at once.

"Right," Mitch said. "Right. But of course it's much harder to do something like that once you start actually fucking."

"Well, one thing that some guys do that I guess must help is to vary the strokes—slowing down and then speeding up, and going in all the way or just a little bit—sometimes with just barely the tip of the cock."

"And doing that also makes it much better for the woman?"

"Exactly! That's just it, Mitch. You can start doing these things for selfish reasons, but they make the sex much better for your partner also. It's like going down on a woman—what you're really doing is getting her much more *ready* and much hotter, so she'll be much better for you. I had a customer once who wanted to fuck and I wasn't quite ready, so I asked him to suck me a little and he said, 'Oh, no, I don't do that. Especially when I'm paying—you're here to please me, not the other way around.' I told him, 'It's not for my benefit, it's for *yours*—it's to lubricate me so I'll be better for you.' But he wouldn't do it, the stupid shmuck, so he got a sandpapery screw."

Mitch chuckled. "Poetic justice! Did he learn his lesson? Did he do it the next time?"

"Next time! There wasn't any next time—I never saw him again. If I don't really like a guy, he never gets to see me a second time—I don't care if he offers me five hundred dollars."

"Well, as your accountant I can't approve of that attitude, but as a friend I think it's great. And I'm glad you want to keep on with our lessons."

I stroked his chest and kissed him. "You're going to *love* the next one."

"Oh, yeah? Oh, come on, now, Barbara, don't tease me like that—tell me what it's going to be."

I couldn't help laughing at his eagerness and curiosity, and decided I had to give him a hint and really let him have something to look forward to. "We're going to give each other some head—but not in the usual places."

Mitch grinned at me with understanding and a mischievous delight. "You mean we're really going to get to the bottom of things."

He made a grab for me and I pulled away, laughing. "Mitch, wait! Not now, next time. You've already made me give it away. Just for that, I'm going to give you a homework assignment—pick up a girl and practice with her."

"I'll try my best. But anyway, let's make our next date on Monday, okay? At seven."

"You've got it. I'll call you at work Monday and confirm."

The lesson on Monday, of course, was rimming, and Mitch got an A-plus on the giving end and an A summa cum laude on the receiving end. I was curious about the homework assignment, but he didn't say anything, so I assumed he hadn't been able to pick anyone up, and I didn't want to make him feel bad by mentioning it. Overall, he was still set to graduate with flying colors.

If Mitch was a good student, so was I, and I lost little time in putting into practice the things Eric had explained to me in the back of Jerry's cab. (It struck me as funny that I had learned more about sex from a homosexual in just one evening than I had learned from a lot of straight guys over affairs that lasted for months. But I think that's because it's somehow easier for people to be much more open about sex when they're talking with someone they know they'll never go to bed with. It shouldn't be that way, but it just is. I guess it's for the same reason that so many guys can be more open with a hooker: there's no emotional stake, no relationship to be put in jeopardy, so there's no fear of putting the other person off.) On my next date with Arnie I decided both to test Eric's prostrate theory and to give Arnie a chance to screw me in the ass for the first time. It could have just as well been Paul or Tony, but I think I picked Arnie because he was the freakiest and because our long talk about rimming had made me feel especially comfortable with him.

I was giving him a tongue bath, and after I had rimmed him and was sucking his cock, I put my finger on his asshole and started stroking it. Then I gently put just the tip in—I

119

wear my fingernails short anyway, so that's no problem—
and waited to see his reaction.

"Ummm," he said. "That feels great. Stick it in some
more."

I pushed my finger in slowly. I wanted to ask Arnie if I
should move it in and out or just leave it there, but I was
having such a great time sucking his cock, I couldn't bear to
take my mouth away to talk. I think Arnie probably sensed
that, because he liked to watch me suck his cock and he
could see how much I was loving it and really getting into it,
and he spoke up as if he could read my mind. "Just move it
around a little bit, slowly." I moved my finger in and out
and back and forth a little, and Arnie began moaning and
groaning; his excitement was exciting me, and I started moving my tongue around the tip of his cock while I continued
to suck him with my lips. Arnie was starting to get carried
away; he could sense how turned on I was and that turned
him on even more. "Oooh, that's beautiful," he said, "but
faster now, faster front and back." I sucked him as hard and
deep as I could and moved my finger in and out like a cock,
and Arnie came explosively, pumping great gobs of hot and
salty come into my mouth. I swallowed it down and licked
him clean and then looked up and grinned at him, and he
reached for me and gave me a big hug and a kiss.

"You are truly fantastic," he said. "I won't ask where
you've been learning all these new tricks, but I can guess."

He was thinking of my other customers, of course, and I
had a sudden vision of him at the gay disco and burst out
laughing. "Your guess is wrong, but I'm not going to tell you
the truth! I'll just let you wonder and wonder."

"Oh, come on, it's an easy guess. There are only two pos-
sibilities: one of your other clients or Kathy—good old
Kathy with her trusty vibrator."

"Her what?"

"Her vibrator. She never told you about that?"

"No. She's told me about everything else, but never that.

The secretive bitch! I can't figure out why she didn't tell me."

Arnie chuckled. "Maybe she wants to keep it as her own personal specialty. Or maybe she didn't want you spending your hard-earned money on one."

"Well, a lot of it is easy-earned money—you know that. But tell me, how does she use it?"

"The favorite way is to stick it up a guy's ass to turn him on or while he's coming—or both. It's thin, you know, and shaped just right, and when it's greased up and going at the slow speed it feels terrific."

"Far-out stuff." I remembered how good Jerry had felt in my ass and had a sudden urgent desire to try the vibrator myself. "I'm going to get one first thing tomorrow."

"Wait a minute now! Don't tell Kathy that I told you about it. I shouldn't be so indiscreet about this stuff—I should have just brought up the vibrator without mentioning Kathy. I don't want to be the cause of any problems between you two."

"Oh, Arnie, don't worry, it'll be all right. I was just kidding before about 'secretive bitch' and all that. We tell each other *everything*. I'm sure the only reason she didn't ever say anything about it is that it never crossed her mind. But if it'll make you feel better, I'll say that one of my other customers, one who doesn't know her, asked me to get one and does she know anything about them."

"Barbara, you're a sweet girl at heart. And when you do get it, I want to be the first to try it out."

"Arnie, you're a *freak* at heart! But I promise, you will be the first."

"Great. And call me soon."

I promised that I would. Arnie and I wished each other sweet dreams, and I was off.

The next day I was hit by a craving for some good French food, so I called Tony and dropped some broad hints about Grenouille.

"What's that, Barbara? You haven't had a really great French meal for quite a while? Well, I know a lovely little place up on the Grand Concourse run by this nice young couple from Algeria—"

"Come *on,* Tony, don't be a tease." Suddenly I remembered Tony asking me for Greek on our first date, and I said, "Take me to Grenouille and we can work on resolving that problem you brought up at our first meeting."

He was stumped for just a moment, but then he perked right up. "Oh, you mean that deal in Greece?"

"Yes, exactly, I do want to pursue that Greek deal."

"Well, that's great—I think it could be very profitable. How about Thursday at six at Grenouille?"

"Tony, do we have to go to the same old place all the time? Don't you like a little variety now and then?"

"Barbara, I have some *sane* clients I have to deal with, so I'll see you Thursday. 'Bye."

I smiled and put the phone back on the hook and at that moment it hit me: I had forgotten to offer Arnie the ass fucking last night! I had gotten so carried away talking about vibrators it had completely slipped my mind. But it could certainly wait until the next time. You may love fourteen dishes on the menu, but you can't have them all at the same meal.

But when I go to Grenouille I'm often tempted to try that anyway. We had another stupefyingly delicious dinner, as always—fresh caviar and Taittinger, roast duckling with green peppercorn sauce and those skinny but incredibly savory French string beans, and a raspberry soufflé. And, as always, Tony and I had a lovely conversation about everything under the sun; dining with him was my escape from everyday cares into this wonderful fantasy world of great food and charm where I could imagine myself leading—if only for a few hours—the warm, secure, leisurely life of the rich.

But after we had finished the duck and were waiting for the soufflé, we started talking about the "Greek deal," and I told Tony all about my initiation and what had led up to it. I could see that the conversation was getting him dangerously excited, even to the point where I was afraid he might want to leave before the soufflé and coffee, so I said I had to go to the ladies' room as an excuse to interrupt the conversation. But Tony said he had to go too, so we left the table and set off together. The toilets are in the very back of the restaurant, in a little hallway in the corner, first the men's and then the women's in the rear wall. Tony had his arm around me and was whispering obscene things in my ear about how expert he was at ass fucking. We paused for just a second while he tried the door to the men's room; it was unlocked and swung open, so I started to continue to the ladies' room, but Tony suddenly pulled his arm tight around me and hauled me into the men's room and locked the door before I knew what was happening.

"Tony!" I said, starting to ask him what the hell he was doing, but he quickly put his hand over my mouth and said, "Shh!" Then he pulled down the toilet seat and sat me down on it, and in a flash I realized what he wanted, but I started laughing so hard I didn't think I'd be able to do it. He just grinned at me and pulled down his pants and shorts; his hard-on was throbbing so hard it was practically bouncing up and down. I thought, *What the hell, if Tony needs some quick relief right here in La Grenouille this is the only possible place—the kitchen is out of the question*—and I stopped laughing long enough to suck Tony off. He was very, very hot and came almost instantly, which was indeed fortunate, because as he was coming someone tried the door. I glanced up at Tony, and my eyebrows shot up as I swallowed his come; the whole thing seemed not at all erotic but screamingly funny.

The guy outside tried the door again and Tony said very politely, "Just a minute," and he lifted his shorts and pants and buckled his belt and gave me his hand to help me up from the seat. We grinned at each other, and Tony opened the door for me. We walked out of there poker-faced as if it were the most normal thing in the world for a man and a woman to go to the men's room at La Grenouille together. The guy waiting outside the door was a young executive type, and for the rest of my life I'll be able to see in my mind's eye the *incredible* mixture of expressions crossing his face: irritation and astonishment and lustful comprehension all mixing in an instant into an indescribable now-I've-seen-everything shock. We turned the corner and entered the dining room and I burst out laughing again, and by the time we got to the table and sat down, the tears were in my eyes and I was afraid I wouldn't be able to stop laughing.

Tony just sat there and grinned like the cat that swallowed the canary. Thankfully, the soufflé came just then, and by concentrating on how scrumptious it looked and watching the captain spoon it out onto plates and ladle out the sauce with fresh whole raspberries, I was able to gradually get myself under control.

I took a bite of soufflé, and the intense warmth and fruity raspberry flavor filled my mouth and made the salty taste of Tony disappear. I swallowed it with delight and relief and glanced at Tony, who was already completely absorbed in his dessert.

"Tony, you are cr-r-razy. *In*-sane. But you're wonderful."

He just grinned again. "You have to be able to do something on impulse once in a while. Not something we'll repeat, certainly, but as a sudden inspiration I consider it dazzling."

"Inspired is the word. Now let's have some coffee, and until we get home maybe we should talk about the, uh, Supreme Court."

We lingered over the café filtre and then took our usual

long walk on the way to Tony's place. It turned out that he hadn't been at all immodest in bragging about how good he was at Greek; he was extremely expert and gentle, and, just as Jerry had, he helped me get ready by rimming me for a long time. I loved it if possible even more than I had with Jerry. It struck me again that often I enjoy the sex so much, I'd jump at the chance for it even if I wasn't being paid.

I was thinking about ass fucking on the way home in the cab, and of course that reminded me of Eric, and I realized how eager I was to see him again. I called him as soon as I got home and he sounded delighted to hear from me.

"Barbara, I'm so glad you called. I've been thinking about you, and I'd love to see you. And it's lucky I'm home for your call—I'm usually out at this hour."

"I know, but I've had a lucky day all around, so I thought I'd press it a little. I was hoping maybe we could have dinner tomorrow or Sunday."

"Sunday is good if we can do it early—and early is better for you anyway, isn't it? And since you're a restaurant fiend like Jerry, I'll let you pick the place—but not too fancy and uptownish, please."

"Well, let's make it Da Silvano. That's in the Village, and it's got a very interesting Italian menu. It's pretty expensive, but—"

"That's okay, we'll go Dutch. This is going to be a very liberated relationship."

"Of course! But let me treat this time and you can treat next time. That's better than doing all the boring arithmetic. Six o'clock?"

"Perfect. See you then, Barbara."

I got to Da Silvano a few minutes early, and Eric was already there, looking very handsome in a crimson shirt unbuttoned almost to his navel and nursing a glass of white wine. I was wearing jeans and an old shirt, and I must admit it was nice for a change to have a date with a man and not worry about looking nice and dressing up.

"Barbara, this was a great idea—my kind of place exactly, small and Villagey and cozy."

"Great—I thought you'd like it. And the food is usually very good and kind of different; it's much more than your basic lasagna-and-veal place."

"Well, that may make it a little advanced for me, but I really do want to learn about food—seeing how much pleasure you and Jerry take in it and how much you know has inspired me. Is that what you do? I mean, are you into food as part of your job—you're a cook or a food editor?"

"No, I wouldn't dare do that; I love it too much, and I'd end up weighing three hundred pounds. I'm just a secretary, but I'm in a nice office with good people and I don't really mind it. And—and I do something else that I don't tell anyone about, but I want to tell you, because I feel I can trust you and I'd like to have the kind of good friendship where we can tell each other anything and everything."

"I'm very good at keeping secrets, and that's exactly the kind of friendship I want too. A woman can be a lot closer to a gay guy because the sex thing isn't there and there are none of those tensions or problems."

"That's what I think too. Though I must admit that with a great-looking young guy like you, we're all tempted to see if we can be the one to turn you around. But I know you don't want that, so I won't try it. Now, the secret is that I'm a part-time call girl."

Eric's face lit up with a mixture of surprise and delight, and he said, "Just like me! That's great! Well, I mean, that's great if you like it. I do—variety and the extra cash."

"That's it—it's not only the money but also this fantastic bonus—I meet fascinating guys like Jerry and they take me to all sorts of fabulous places that I probably would never get to otherwise. And"—I smiled into his eyes—"I meet a lot of wonderful people that way. If I wasn't seeing Jerry, I would never have gotten to know you."

Eric beamed at me and then turned thoughtful. "The way I do it doesn't usually bring those kinds of benefits, but that's because I can't do it your way. A lot of my customers are straight, and I'm a totally *secret* sin for them—they can't let *anyone* know. But anyway, let's order, and then you can tell me all about it, and maybe I'll see what I can use and apply for myself." He grinned. "A professional symposium."

Eric asked me to order for him, and I suggested we share single portions of several dishes so he could taste more things. We split a seafood salad, two pasta dishes—gnocchi and the spaghetti in anchovy and olive sauce—and a veal chop in white wine sauce, with a bottle of white Corvo. It didn't sound like that much when I ordered, but it added up to a lot, and by the time we got to dessert we just had room for melon. It was a delicious meal, though, and Eric enjoyed the food and asked questions about it; I could see that this was going to develop as another shared interest. And in between I told him all about my new life and how it had awakened me sexually but sometimes overloaded me emotionally. He listened with loads of understanding and sympathy, and it felt marvelous to have someone who wasn't involved who I could pour everything out to.

Over the espresso I said, "But we've spent this whole dinner talking about me. Now I want to hear about you—where you come from, how you spend all that wonderful free time, what you want to be."

"Wow. My whole life story. I'm twenty-one, and I was brought up on Long Island by loving, wealthy, and very conventional parents. I went to the Lawrenceville School and was the perfect preppie until I seduced a very appealing-looking freshman and got caught one night giving him a *terrific* blow job. I don't mean to be immodest, Barbara, but it really was, it was—well, let's not digress too much. Anyhow, my parents were informed, and my father had a fit of self-righteous rage and disgust and said he didn't want a *faggot* for a son and wouldn't support me anymore. I was still not eighteen, so I guess legally I could have forced him to support me, but I thought, *Screw it, it's not worth the hassle and embarrassment.* My mother usually tried to soften the effects of my father's more extreme hangups, but this time she was pretty disturbed herself that her only son had turned out to be queer. But she did slip me three thousand bucks to get myself lauched on my own, so I got my stuff together and headed for the Village, where at least I felt at home. I got a decent and reasonable walk-up in one of those old tenements, and before long I discovered that a good-looking, slim, and *young* gay guy was exactly what a lot of very civilized and very wealthy men were looking for —and that I could easily get $250 for a trick without having to hustle any sleazoids. Then one night in one of the bars, I met this guy who works on Wall Street and makes pots of money. He lives in Morristown with his wife and kids and he, like, keeps me. He pays the rent and buys me clothes and throws me a couple of hundred now and then, and I entertain him once or twice a week. And of course he has the first call on my time, ahead of my other customers. Otherwise, I love to listen to jazz and go to the clubs, and to stay up all night dancing and getting high. I'm really perfectly happy with this life, but Jerry very definitely thinks I should get a job. He says that otherwise when I get too old to sell myself I'll turn into a bum—and beyond that he just generally feels that everyone should work. I think in a way he's right, but I really don't know what I want to do or learn to do, and I'm just having too goddamn much fun now to really worry about it."

"Yeah. You're both right—you and Jerry. Your life now is too easy to give up, but a job would give you some stability, some base, you know? And you need to be able to do something to get through life—you can't go on like this forever."

"I know, but I always think, *Next month, next year, I'll*

start getting myself together. But you know one thing I'd like to do in the meantime?"

"Be a model? I think you could be one, Eric—it's something you're able to do, it's good money, and it's not a nine-to-five kind of thing that you'd hate and that would cramp your lifestyle."

"No, that's not what I had in mind. But that is a good idea, come to think of it—I would like that. But I was thinking that I'd appreciate it if you could ask your customers if they'd like me to come along with you sometime."

"Oh, God, I don't think any of them would want to. They're all straight guys."

Eric smiled patiently. "Barbara, I don't think you understand. A lot of straight guys have this secret fantasy of being serviced by a gay man, but they're afraid to do it because they're embarrassed and worried that someone might find out, or that they might like it too much and discover that they're really bi. But if they pay for it, that helps make it all right, and if they take only the active role they don't feel like they're queer. And if the gay guy comes along as an add-on, just a little extra twist when they're basically seeing a woman, then they feel really safe, so it's easy for them to go for it that way."

"You sound like you've done this before."

"No—you're the first professional, or semiprofessional, lady I've met. But I just know, I really do—I understand the psychology of the straight male. But now look, Barbara, if you don't want to do this or feel it might screw up your own thing, then don't do it. I'm not going to press you about it—and I wouldn't ask you to press your customers. I just thought that if you want, you might casually say, 'I know this gay guy who'd like to come along and join us, if you want,' and just see what the reaction is. No hard sell at all."

"Well, sure, I could do that. And if they say no, I'll just let it drop. But why do you want to do this?"

"I could use the extra cash, of course, and I get a special

kick out of seducing straight men—I think most of us do. And I'd like to meet these guys anyway—you make them sound so interesting. And I just think that you and I would work very well together."

"I'll give it a try, Eric, and we'll see what happens. I always say I'll try anything once. But how much are you going to ask for?"

"That's up to you—I don't want to screw up your thing, and I certainly don't want you to end up with less money because they're holding to a total amount. So you can set that yourself—fifty or seventy-five. And if you can fix it so you get a cut of that, so much the better. However you want to work it out."

"Okay—I'll let you know what happens. Now, how about a little music? I brought along that jazz club listing from *The New Yorker,* and just about any place you want to go is fine with me."

"I'd really rather show you my record collection. I've got zillions of records and tapes I never seem to listen to enough, and you can check out whichever ones you want."

I laughed, and Eric looked puzzled. "That's funny because it sounds so exactly like a *line*—a line a straight guy would use to try to get me back to his apartment. With you, I know it's not, of course, but the words are so precisely the same, it's just funny. No, I'd love to."

Eric's place was three flights up in an old Village building, but it was very homey and comfortable, with sturdy old furniture, an elaborate stereo system, and bookshelves lined row upon row with hundreds of jazz records and tapes. Not a book in sight, but the whole range of jazz from 1920s Louis Armstrong all the way to Henry Threadgill and other avant-garde and far-out players. We spent a lovely relaxed time listening and talking about the music until I happened to glance at my watch and saw that it was almost eleven o'clock; it felt like about forty minutes had gone by, but we had been there for three hours. "Yipes! Eric, I've got to go to work tomorrow, so I've got to split this instant."

He grimaced. "You day people give me a pain. The evening has barely started."

"Oh, come on, you want to go out to get your kicks anyway. I'll call you soon—at nine in the morning to get you up and out into something respectable."

"I'd forgive you anything," Eric said, giving me a hug and a peck on the cheek.

I was a little reluctant to make good on my promise to mention Eric to customers, but I thought, *What the hell, the worst that can happen is that they'll say no, and if I put it the right way, they're not going to get insulted or angry.* But which one should it be? Jerry was obviously out of the question, and Mitch was certainly nowhere near ready for this and might think that I had some doubts about him; I didn't want to risk undoing all his progress. That left Tony, Arnie, or Paul, and even though I thought Paul was the least likely of the three, I was overdue to see him and thought I might as well give it a whirl.

When I called Paul at his city apartment to set up a date, we made small talk for a minute or two and then decided that I'd come over to his place at six thirty.

"That's a little earlier than usual," Paul said. "Is that all right for you?"

"Oh, sure—as a matter of fact, it's perfect, because I'm going to meet a friend later and he also lives in the Village."

"Aha. Sounds like a new boyfriend."

"No, actually he's gay. A very nice young guy named Eric. I can bring him along if you'd like; I'm sure he'd love to freak off with us."

I said this just a bit tentatively and timidly, and I was astonished by Paul's reaction.

"Oh, *yeah!* Does he like to get fucked?"

"Sure," I said. It took me just a moment to recover from

my surprise at Paul's enthusiasm, and then I started sounding very seductive. "He'll do anything you want—suck your ass and everything."

"Fantastic. Bring him along. How much do I have to give him?"

"Oh, a hundred, I guess. But you know I'm charging an extra thirty-five dollars now if you come twice, so if that applies we can take that out of the hundred."

"That's fine, Barbara. See you tomorrow at six thirty."

When I called Eric, he was delighted but said he wasn't at all surprised at Paul's enthusiasm. When I told him about the financial arrangements, he said he'd certainly let me have the thirty-five dollars and would be happy to give me half of the hundred if Paul came only once—which Eric immodestly thought was most unlikely.

"Eric, *no,* I don't want to take any of your money. We're doing this because we're friends, and if you're going to get into shares and percentages and all that, then I don't want to do it at all. I just gave him back the extra thirty-five on an impulse, and if this gets to be a regular thing we can probably tack that back on top for me. But whatever you get is all yours, period, and I don't want to hear any more about it."

Eric laughed and said that since I was being so nice he wouldn't argue, and he asked me for Paul's address. I told him that I thought it would be much better if we arrived at the same time and that I would pick him up at his place at around six fifteen and we could walk over. Eric wanted to take me to dinner afterward, so I made a reservation for eight o'clock at Raoul's in SoHo.

When we arrived, Paul had taken his usual shower, but this time he was back in the bathrobe. I introduced him to Eric, and they shook hands cordially like two guys meeting at a country club, then Paul asked us to sit down and offered us a drink. Since it was still before dinner for Eric and me, we both had white wine, and Paul joined us.

"Thanks," Eric said when Paul handed him the glass, "and thanks for inviting me along."

Paul beamed at him and said, "It is of course absolutely my pleasure," and they both laughed at the pun. It seemed like they were going to get along famously.

"You know," Paul said conversationally, as if he were talking about sports with an old friend, "this has been a secret fantasy of mine for a long time—especially since Barbara is reluctant to get into the Greek bit."

I couldn't help laughing, and I said, "It's very funny this should happen just now, because it's just now that I'm starting to get into it."

Paul laughed appreciatively at the irony and said, "Such is life; don't things always work out that way? Well, let's go on to my boudoir and get comfortable." Paul put down his glass and stood up and offered each of us a hand, and we walked into the bedroom holding hands as if we'd been a comfy old ménage à trois for months and months.

Paul took off his bathrobe and tossed it onto a chair and lay down on the bed, and of course he had a huge hard-on. Eric looked at it hungrily as he was taking off his clothes and said, "Wow, you've got a *big* cock," and he and Paul looked at each other and laughed as if at a private joke. For a second I felt almost like a fifth wheel, and I said jokingly, "You guys make me feel almost like I'm intruding on your little male scene."

Paul watched me step out of my panties and said with mock concern, "Oh, now, Barbara, don't pout—come over here and help us get freaky."

Eric, who had a hard-on himself, lay down beside Paul and began licking and sucking his armpit, reaching down to fondle his cock, and I licked his balls and his thighs. I was surprised at what a turn-on it was to watch Eric's mouth and tongue working on Paul; he sucked the other armpit, then licked Paul's neck and chest and sucked his nipples. Paul lifted his ass off the bed so I could rim him, and Eric moved down to suck his cock. "Oooh, that's perfect," Paul said with a moan; "a guy really knows how to do it."

After a minute or so, Eric gave Paul's cock a few last licks and said to me, "Let's switch." Paul went over on his side and he and I did a sixty-nine while Eric sucked his asshole; Paul was getting frantic, and his tongue was going up and down my clit like mad. He pulled away after a while, and Eric lay face down on the bed with his ass poking up invitingly over the edge; he knew exactly what Paul wanted. Paul stood behind Eric and slowly eased his cock into Eric's ass, and Eric groaned with pleasure. I knelt behind Paul and sucked his ass while he fucked Eric; it was a little hard at first because he was moving, but I soon got into the rhythm of his motion. "Oh, *God,* that feels so great," Paul said, and he started moving faster and faster, and I could feel his ass contract as he came inside Eric. Paul pulled out slowly, and as I stood up I saw Eric roll over on his back and start playing with his hard-on. He and Paul both had kind of wild, dazed expressions, and I could tell that Paul was still in a frantic state. He stared at Eric's cock for a moment then suddenly knelt down and began licking it. Eric took his hand away and lay back and played with his own nipples, and Paul began sucking his cock. I was watching, entranced, and suddenly I realized how much I wanted a hard cock up my pussy at that moment, but I knew this was not the time and tried to push the desire away. Paul was getting another hard-on, and for a second I thought he wanted to make Eric come in his mouth, but he pulled away and reached for me and said, "Are you really ready? I want to be the man in the middle."

"Oh, yeah," I said, hugging Paul and giving him a deep French kiss. Then I lay down on the bed, and Paul slowly stuck his cock in my ass; there was that first brief moment of pain and then it felt marvelous. Paul grunted and jerked forward as Eric entered him, and the two of them moved slowly at first, their rhythms matching perfectly; it seemed as if I could feel Eric moving inside Paul. They started moving faster and faster, and I could feel Paul coming inside me, then a few seconds later jerking forward convulsively as Eric came inside him. They slowly came to a stop, but then they both kind of relaxed and let their weight fall on me, and I went, "Oomph! Hey!" and they got up quickly.

"Sorry," Paul said. "I got a little carried away."

"You sure did!" Eric said, giving him an affectionate pat on the back, then looking at me with concern and saying, "Are you all right?"

"I'll be okay. Just give me a minute to catch my breath." I felt exhausted, and the desire for an ordinary fuck had disappeared.

Paul excused himself for another quick shower and Eric grinned at me and said, "Fantastic." I smiled back and said, "Beyond all our wildest dreams." Eric started to get dressed, and a minute later I felt better and started putting my clothes on.

We went into the living room, and soon Paul came to join us, wrapped in a big red towel and carrying a wad of cash. He gave each of us $185 and said, "Forgive my generosity, but I had an unbelievable time, and somehow it just doesn't seem fair to me to give one of you more than the other."

"We'll forgive you *this time,*" Eric said, and we all laughed. Eric and I thanked him, and we all agreed that we had to do this again sometime, and Eric and I left for dinner at Raoul's.

We were both a little beat, so we gave up our plans for a long walk and grabbed a cab.

"I'm amazed," I said. "I never thought he'd go that far."

"Neither did I—I thought he'd just want to take the active part. But he really got into it. It'll be interesting to see if he gets hooked."

"I kind of doubt it. I think it may have been just a once-in-a-lifetime thing—I mean, the passive side, anyway. But I will suggest you for next time, and I'll bounce you off two of my other guys and see if they're interested."

We pulled up at Raoul's, and Eric looked at it and said, "Is *this* the place? It looks like a bar."

"You're in for a surprise, Eric!" And I couldn't resist driving home the point by ordering a very French meal for him: poached leeks vinaigrette and then sweetbreads. I thought maybe I was pushing his culinary education too fast, but I was the one who got the surprise; he not only loved it but also sampled my snails and duck with great gusto.

"You're a natural-born teacher, Barbara. You know when to go slow and when to shove your student into the water and let him sink or swim." I thought that if he and Mitch both thought I was a good teacher, maybe I did have some talent and should think about trying to develop it. I didn't tell Eric about Mitch, but I said that maybe I'd start toying with the idea of becoming a professional teacher. We had a long discussion about it, but Eric discouraged me by pointing out that it would require a lot of preparation I didn't have time for and that having summers off would probably tempt me to get into too much mischief.

Eric wanted to top the evening off at a jazz club, but I begged off, saying I was too tired and had to get up for work the next day. So we got a cab and I dropped Eric off at his place on my way uptown.

After that evening I thought I'd done everything, but there was still more to come. A few weeks later I had a date with Jerry, and we went to Plato's Retreat.

I was surprised at how big the place was; the club was housed in a building that was far west on Thirty-fourth Street and could have been a convention hall. The locker and bathroom area alone was bigger than all of Le Trapeze, and when you came out after checking your clothes there was a seemingly endless warren of semiprivate swing rooms, a disco dance floor that looked half the size of a football field, a game room with pool tables, a big swimming pool, a whirlpool bath, a large open orgy room, and several movie rooms. Jerry took me on a quick tour of the whole place, and then we went for a swim and followed that up with a dip in the whirlpool; I was having loads of fun and I hadn't even touched anyone yet. It was a Friday night, and there were hundreds of people there, most of them young and great-looking.

Jerry and I dried off and went to the orgy room. We walked around enjoying the show. In one corner a beautiful black girl was being eaten out by a young blond woman; the black girl had lovely big erect tits, and I knew I recognized her—it was Lillian, the charmer we had met at the gay disco. Jerry caressed my ass and smiled at me and said, "I just had a feeling we'd run into her tonight."

We went over and sat down next to Lillian, and she recognized us immediately. She gave us a sensual smile and said "Hi!" and we could tell she was too turned on for mere conversation. She reached for me without further ado and guided me so I was sitting over her face. I slowly lowered my pussy into her mouth, and Jerry started sucking her breasts. Lillian had the warmest, softest, most educated and fantastic tongue I had ever felt, man or woman, and she was getting me hotter and hotter by the second. I watched the blonde turning Lillian on the same way and Jerry sucking and squeezing her tits, and that got me even more excited, and soon I was coming, in a long, slow, delicious release.

Lillian continued to suck me, until I got to the point where I couldn't take any more, so I shifted forward so she could stick that incredible tongue up my ass. By this time Lillian was coming herself, her hips and her whole body writhing. All I could think of was how much I wanted her, and I climbed off and kissed her; her tongue went everywhere in my mouth and she stroked my breasts. Jerry and the blonde saw what was happening and moved away, reaching for each other; they got into a sixty-nine as I started sucking Lillian's tits, rolling my tongue around her huge, hard nipples.

Then I went down and sucked her pussy. I thought, *This is the first time for me but it feels as if I've been doing it for years.* Lillian was juicy and hot and tasted wonderful, and an ecstatic feeling of great warmth and tenderness came over me as I lovingly sucked her clit and tongued her cunt. A slim, bearded black guy, apparently Lillian's friend, came up behind me and began sucking my pussy and ass. I made Lillian come again for a long time, and then the black guy and Jerry both reached for me at once.

"I want you both!" I said frantically, pushing Jerry down and climbing on top of his hard-on. I lay flat on him and sucked his armpits, and the black guy eased his cock into my ass. It was an incredible sensation, even better and more intense than the coke rush, feeling both cocks moving inside me at the same time. They both came at once, and I felt as if I was being lifted up in the air and floating twenty feet above the mattress. I was carried away in a kind of wild double orgasm, in my ass and my cunt at the same time, and I came close to blacking out with the intensity of the pleasure. The black guy pulled out, and I rolled off Jerry and flopped down next to him with my arm around his chest, holding on to kind of steady myself until I could come back into the world.

Lillian came over and kissed me, then the black guy did the same, and they smiled at Jerry and me and said, "It was great—see you next time." I wanted to say, "Wait! We want to party with you all the time, at our house!" but Jerry just said, "Good night, take care," and Lillian and her friend walked off, holding hands.

I turned to Jerry and said, "Wouldn't you love to set up regular dates with them—at your place, or theirs?"

"Oh, I'd love to, Barbara—I'd *love* to have her. But it's just not done at these places; it's not the etiquette. You don't make outside dates with people you meet here—you can hope to swing with them again here, and if you get to know them well you can even make plans to come on the same night. But you never ask to see anyone on a private basis. It's like that blonde; after we finished our sixty-nine, she just said goodnight and split for someone else."

"Well, I don't see why you can't set up meetings privately —if you really like them, and they like you."

"It has to do with maintaining everyone's privacy and freedom and anonymity—you don't ask for anyone's address or phone number or last name or anything like that. This way you can feel freer, and there aren't any problems of trust that come up."

"I see—I get it. But I'm still disappointed!"

"You don't have to be. We'll see them again here, or maybe we'll run into them at Trapeze."

"I hope so. You want to get into some more freakouts here, or are you ready to split?"

"Are you kidding? First that blonde and then our threeway—I am *through* for the night."

I laughed. "Me too. I think a quick dip in the pool would refresh us just right and then we can go."

"I'm with you," Jerry said. We swam for only a couple of minutes, just enough to perk ourselves up. Then Jerry drove me over to Third Avenue to get a cab, giving me a hundred fifty dollars on the way, and we made our usual plans for me to call him in a few days.

I felt I needed to talk to someone about all this wild new stuff I'd been getting into, to help me absorb the impact of it all and reassure myself I wasn't turning into a complete freak, so I called Kathy the next day and we made a dinner date for Sunday at Gino's. I also wanted to ask her about the vibrator bit, but I didn't mention that on the phone.

The crowds at Gino's are usually worse when Bloomingdale's, just down the street, is open late, but sometimes on Sundays it's even more packed, and this was one of those times. We had to wait about forty minutes for a table, so we hung out at the bar drinking daiquiris, two apiece, and by the time we sat down we were well-oiled for a serious talk.

We had arugula salads and the chicken with garlic and we split—supposedly against our better judgment—a bottle of Soave. I told Kathy all about doing the Greek and Eric—without, of course, identifying Jerry or Paul—and my first full lesbian trip with the black girl and getting screwed in the cunt and the ass at the same time.

"Barbara, this is all perfectly normal—if that's the right word! I guess it's not, but you know what I mean—this is what happens, you broaden your sexual horizons and you get freer and wilder. Sometimes I think every girl should do this just to get awakened sexually! But seriously, since you enjoyed it, and no harm came, it's great. There's nothing to worry about as long as you don't get into any sick or dangerous shit like S&M or getting tied up and all that."

"Oh, God, no, I'd never do that. I won't even do pictures or movies. One guy wanted to take pictures of me and videotapes of the two of us in action. He offered to let me wear a mask, but I said, 'No way, I'm not going to do it, not even if you give me five hundred bucks,' and I never saw him again after that."

"Well, as long as you've got your limits and you stick to them, no problem."

"Right. There is one other thing, but I guess it might be okay. One of my guys wants me to bring along a vibrator."

Kathy giggled. "Oh, that can be fun. I've got one, and I can lend it to you. Or you can buy one—you can even get them now in respectable department stores. You have to be a little careful, and you can't use it in the shower and electrocute everybody, but it's basically harmless. And it comes in especially handy when a guy can't get it up. You just give him a little rectal massage and that almost always works."

"Kathy, you're great—you ought to do a TV show on sex, with people calling in and all that."

"Maybe someday. When I retire! Now let's get some

cheesecake with strawberries on it and coffee and you can tell me more about this gay guy. That's something new to *me*."

"Well, like I said, he's a very sweet guy and a good friend. But it turned out that it was just this one customer who wanted to see him. When I suggested him to the others, they were turned off by the idea. Eric says almost all straight guys have this secret fantasy of making it with a guy, but I don't think that's necessarily true."

"I don't either, but Eric does sound nice. I'd like to meet him someday."

"Sure. He's a steak-and-potatoes type now, but I'm turning him on to food."

Kathy and I started discussing our weight problems even as we were savoring our cheesecake and strawberries, and that started us on clothes, and the whole sex thing was left behind. But I felt tremendously better for having talked to her about my escapades; it always gives me a wonderfully secure feeling and peace of mind to have someone I can really confide in.

The next day on my lunch hour I went out and bought a vibrator, and when I started to use it I saw that Kathy had been absolutely right about its being a big help when a guy can't get a hard-on. This happens every once in a while with almost everyone; he's too tired or he's had too much to drink or he's just been having too much sex in the last few days.

When this happens, I'm always careful to be very understanding and *patient* and not in the least bit threatening. Putting the vibrator up his ass does work almost all the time; if he doesn't like that or I don't have it, I can usually get results by using my finger instead to massage inside his ass or by rimming him a lot. Another technique that almost always works is to massage his cock with that K-Y lubricating jelly. Sometimes, if it's a guy who especially loves to go down on me, I'll ask him to eat me for a long time, telling him how great he is at it, and usually when he sees how much I love it he'll get hard as a rock.

As a last resort, I'll use speed if I have it. Jerry turned me on to it, and I like only a very *little* bit and only occasionally, because otherwise it makes me too jumpy and nervous. But Jerry told me he likes it because it makes him extra horny, and I've discovered that if a guy is willing to try a little, it can give him a raging hard-on.

So with one thing or another, I help the guy out and there is, as they say, *no problem!*

V. Leading a Double Life

Actually, my biggest problem in being a part-time call girl has nothing to do with sex. It's the constant strain of keeping the work secret and the constant fear that someone—especially my parents or the people at work—is going to find out.

I'm most terrified of my parents ever discovering what I do; they're so religious and old-fashioned that they'd be enormously hurt and angry. I usually see them only on Thanksgiving and Christmas, and in between we'll talk on the phone a few times a month, so usually there are no problems. But when I got my new apartment on the East Side, they came over to see it and I had a few tense moments.

When I told them that I was moving, they said they wanted to see the place—"a kind of housewarming," as my mother put it—so I said that as soon as I had a chance to get it furnished and put in proper shape, I'd have them over for a Sunday dinner. That gave me time to get my alibis in order: I'd gotten a raise; I felt so much safer there than on Amsterdam Avenue that the new apartment was worth the higher rent just for that; I was saving money by not eating out so much and by buying fewer clothes and by not taking cabs unless it was absolutely necessary.

I wanted to make them a really nice meal, so I went out Sunday morning and bought asparagus and other vegetables and some good tuna and prosciutto for an antipasto, and raspberries for dessert with some of that wonderful Reggiano Parmesan, the real stuff, and a chicken and mushrooms and tomatoes and all the rest of the fixings for a chicken cacciatore. It wasn't until I got the food home and set it out on the kitchen counter that it hit me. I was admiring the asparagus and the beautiful raspberries and I suddenly realized what I had done. *You idiot,* I thought, *how can anyone be so goddamn stupid; you got a whole collection of very expensive foods—the best prosciutto and Parmesan and asparagus and raspberries.* I was so angry with myself, I was tempted to pick it all up and hurl it out the window. I could have gotten beans and escarole and pears with a little Fontina cheese, and my parents would have been just as pleased and would see that I was economizing. Instead, I was practically advertising how much cash I had to throw around. I stood there and gripped the edge of the counter hard with both hands to try to control myself and thought, *You dumb shit, save the chicken for Monday and go get a filet of beef and some foie gras and truffles for a sauce.*

When I calmed down I thought, *Well, it's done, it's too late now, so let's think about how we can explain this.* The dinner was a special occasion; I hadn't cooked for my parents for a very long time, and I wanted to make an especially wonderful meal. And that was absolutely true, so there'd be no problem at all making it sound convincing. And I could go get one of those $1.98 bottles of second-rate Soave and say I had wanted to get a better wine but had run out of money. Then I remembered that you can't buy wine on Sunday, and I thought bitterly that maybe being a part-time call girl was starting to damage my brain cells. I went to the closet and looked in the corner where I keep my wine and there were two bottles of Antinori Chianti and a bottle of good French Chablis. The Chianti was less expensive and would go better anyway, and I could say I had gotten it as a gift. That's it—someone had given me the Chianti, and the Parmesan too. *Of course it's a gift, Mother; you know I can't afford to spend fifteen dollars a pound just for a grating and dessert cheese.* I took the Chianti to the kitchen, thinking that maybe my brain was still working after all, and started preparing the meal.

My parents came promptly at one o'clock, and after the hugs and kisses we sat down at the table.

"Barbara," my mother said, "it's a wonderful apartment and a fine building, but isn't this neighborhood awfully expensive?"

I laughed. "That's why this place is so small!"

"How much is it, Barbara?" my father asked seriously.

He looked so concerned that I just couldn't bring myself to say "six hundred." "Five hundred." It was such a small lie, a hundred-dollar lie, a fifteen percent lie, but still my heart sped up and I could feel myself tensing.

"Five hundred!" he said. "That's a lot! What were you paying at the old place—two eighty-five?"

"Yeah, but, Dad, I just didn't feel *safe* there." This was my trump card, appealing to their fears about my safety, and I decided to give it the full treatment. "This neighborhood is so much better; if I come home late at night from a date or something, I don't have to worry. The things that used to go on over there, the muggings and knifings and all that, they just don't happen around here. I think that's worth any amount of money, to feel safe and not to worry."

"Well," my father said, "we think so too, we want you safe, but that's still an awful lot of money. How can you afford it?"

"They're supposed to give me a raise pretty soon at work —Mr. Allen has promised it to me. I've been there a long time, you know, and I'm sure they'll come through with it soon. And I'm just going to have to cut back on the eating out and the clothes, and not take a cab unless it's very late or freezing. But you know, it's that expression they have here in Manhattan—'rent poor.' Everybody here is rent poor. You have to pay a fortune to get anything decent. It's not like the Bronx, where you can get a big apartment for three or four hundred."

"But," my mother said, "that's just it, Barbara. We've always said you could move—"

I interrupted her, delighted to have the change of subject. "Oh, no—no way! I'm not going to go live up there again and ride that stinking subway back and forth every day. Uh-unh. I go to and from work on the bus now, and at least it's a civilized experience."

I managed to keep the discussion away from my finances for a while, but when I served dessert I just knew what my mother was going to say, and I sure wasn't disappointed.

"Barbara, this was a lovely meal, and the Chianti was wonderful, but it shows the same kind of extravagance that made you get the apartment. Prosciutto, asparagus, raspberries, the best Parmesan—this dinner must have cost you a fortune."

"I know, Mother, but this is the first time in ages that I've cooked a meal for you and Dad, and I wanted to make it really special. And it's not as bad as it seems—the wine and the Parmesan were gifts, and of course chicken is cheap. But don't worry! Next time I have you over, you'll probably be lucky to get a bean casserole with a little chopped meat in it and a banana to share for dessert!"

They smiled, but I could tell they were still worried, and I was getting more and more on edge. I wanted to put the whole thing to rest once and for all, so I said, "Don't worry about me. I'm going to be all right. If worst comes to worst, I can always work on Saturdays; there's always demand for a good secretary part-time. But I'm not going to come running to you for help and a loan here and a loan there—don't worry about that."

This made Dad get very serious and paternal, and he said, "It's not a question of that, Barbara—you know you can always come to us for help when you need it. And of course we understand why you want a nice place; we just think you may have gotten in a little over your head."

Suddenly I had an inspiration, and I said lightly. "Someday I'll get married and my rent costs will go down to zero!" and this had exactly the effect I intended: it set my mother off and running on her favorite topic in the whole world, when is Barbara going to get married and how is Barbara getting along with Michael and is it really a serious relationship and on and on, and that took care of the conversation for the rest of their visit.

I was relieved when it was over. It had been a very tense afternoon for me, and I hadn't enjoyed the meal. But I realized that I was going to have to quiet my parents' concern and prevent them from becoming suspicious, and that the way to do that was to play the role of Miss Thrifty to the hilt. So now every time I talk to them, I try to slip in some comment about how I'm saving money, by getting a boyfriend to take me to dinner more often or making do with an old coat or living for a week on tuna and pasta. And so far, thank God, it seems to be working.

It's been fairly easy to make sure that no one at work suspects anything. I've had one very scary close call, but that happened outside the office and had nothing to do with carelessness on my part. None of my customers know where I work, and I never use the phone in the office to call anybody; I either run downstairs and use a pay phone or call on my lunch hour. And I learned the hard way not to do any dates during the day. I called Arnie once to set up a date for his day off, hoping he'd invite me to an early dinner, but he said he was busy that evening and talked me into coming up to see him on my lunch hour. Was that ever a mistake. The sex was rushed, and I got back to work fifteen minutes late. I didn't even have time to get something to eat; I just grabbed a candy bar and a bag of peanuts at the newsstand in the building on my way back in. If I hadn't been lucky in getting a cab right outside Arnie's building, I would have been even later. Nobody said anything, because otherwise I'm always very prompt, but I decided then and there that I would never again do a lunch date.

The close call came one night at Plato's with Jerry. We had already done our thing, and I was sitting in the whirlpool relaxing. Suddenly I heard someone say, "Why, hello, Barbara!" I turned around and there was David, one of the young guys in the office.

"Uh, oh, hi, David. How are you?"

He smiled at my embarrassment and my lame formality. We were both leaning against the side of the whirlpool, and thankfully the water came up to our armpits. If I had been standing in front of him stark naked, with him naked too, it would have been much worse.

"Just great! I must admit I'm a little surprised to see you here. How do you like it?"

"I hate it!" I said convincingly; I was able to make all my nervousness come out as disgust. Then the thought flashed through my mind that maybe David had been in the orgy room and had seen me rimming and going down on men and women and getting fucked every which way—obviously loving it, not hating it—and I realized it would be a fatal mistake to overplay my hand. "I let this guy talk me into coming here, and then I let myself get carried away and act like some crazy nympho and now I'm so disgusted with myself I feel like sliding under this water and staying there."

"Well, I'm really sorry you feel that way. I was hoping, you know, that we—"

I knew what he was going to say, and I suddenly put my hands over my eyes and shook my head like I was going to burst out sobbing, and luckily it worked. He had enough decency or whatever to be embarrassed and sorry. He put his hand lightly on my shoulder and said, "I'm sorry, Barbara. I didn't mean to make it worse for you. Don't cry. I can see you don't belong in this place."

Jerry was in the swimming pool, and I was terrified that he was going to come over and say something to me that would give my whole game away. I felt an urgent need to get away from David fast.

"David, I'm sorry, but I'm too embarrassed to talk to you anymore, and I want to get out of here. But I have to ask you to please do me one favor."

He could see that I was really distraught, and I think he was a little frightened that I'd become completely hysterical. He said comfortingly, "Sure, Barbara. Anything you ask."

I looked into his eyes beseechingly and said, "David, please don't ever tell anyone at work that I was here. I couldn't bear it—I couldn't face them—I wouldn't be able to stay there anymore. I've been there a long time, and I couldn't bear to lose it all just because of this one night. Please?"

"Oh, no, Barbara, I never would. I'll never mention it to anyone. I promise."

"David, thank you. Thanks so much." I got up, ran the few steps to the swimming pool, jumped in, and found Jerry, lazily stroking back and forth. I pulled him over to the side.

"Jerry, we've got to get out of here. Now. Quick."

He took one look at my face, and he could tell that I was in no way kidding. He took my hand without saying a word and helped me out of the pool and led us straight to the lockers. We got dressed in about thirty seconds flat, still not saying a word, and hurried out to his cab.

Jerry started the car and took off fast down Thirty-fourth Street, running the light at Eighth Avenue, and didn't speak until he had to stop for the light at Sixth.

"What's the matter? Did someone threaten you?"

"No. Worse than that."

"Worse! They hit you?"

"No. I ran into one of the guys from my office."

"That's all? From the look on your face, I thought you were in physical danger. You looked absolutely terrified."

"I was. And it's not 'that's all.' That's just what I need, for them to find out and fire me."

"But he doesn't know there's money involved! He doesn't know you're moonlighting as a call girl. Just because you go to Plato's doesn't mean anything. I can see how it could be a little embarrassing, but it doesn't mean anyone's going to find out."

"Well, yeah, I guess you're right. But I didn't stop to think about that; I just panicked. And it *is* dangerous. I don't know whether he saw me in the orgy room or not, but if he did he's probably not going to believe what I told him. I said it was my first time at Plato's, and I got carried away and hated what I did and was ashamed and all that. But even if he does believe it, it just puts me in a totally wrong light, and it's the first seed for them to get suspicious—the first little opening. I've blown enough secrets to know that that's all it takes, that first little pinprick of information, and before you know it the whole thing is out."

"Barbara, calm down. Take a deep breath and just try to relax. You're blowing this all out of proportion. Even if he does tell everyone in your office, 'I saw Barbara at Plato's Retreat doing this and this and that,' there's still no connection with being paid. Lots of straight people go to those places, and everybody has a private life that's much racier and freer than the image they project in the office, in a business situation. No one's going to ostracize you and start watching your every move. And besides, if this guy has any sense of decency at all, he's not going to blab it all over the office. At worst, he may tell it confidentially to one or two guys in the men's room, and they'll keep it to themselves."

"He promised me he wouldn't tell anyone. And I don't think he will; he's not a bad sort."

"Okay! So that's it. You've got nothing to worry about."

I thought for a minute, and I had to admit that Jerry was right. "All right," I said. "I see what you mean. It's not that bad, but it did scare me, and I don't want to let it happen again if I can help it. But if this guy goes to Plato's fairly often, and he sees me there again, that's really going to blow it."

"That's no problem. I like Le Trapeze better anyway, and you like it better, so from now on we'll go there. Hell, the only reason we go to Plato's anyway is for the swimming pool and a little variety. If I really want to go there once in a while, I can take someone else, and I know you're not going to miss it."

"I sure won't. I can go swimming anywhere."

Jerry had turned up Madison Avenue, and by this time we were already at Fifty-fifth Street.

"Jerry, where are we going? Aren't you going to drop me off on Third someplace?"

"I thought we'd go to the Carlyle and have a drink and listen to a little piano, to help you relax and cheer you up a bit. But if you'd rather just head home, of course I can drop you anywhere on Third."

"No, that's a good idea. I'd like that. I could use a drink, and I've never been to the Carlyle."

Jerry paid me before we got out of the cab, and we had Delamain and spent a pleasant hour listening to the music and discussing the superior facilities and classier people at Le Trapeze. Then I got a cab and headed home, reflecting that even if I wasn't a part-time call girl, I still would have been embarrassed to run into David at Plato's. But then I realized that if it weren't for being a part-timer, I probably never would have gotten to Plato's, because I wouldn't have wanted to go and would never have discovered how wonderful it was.

There's been one other incident involving the office, but it was relatively minor and nowhere near as sudden or uncomfortable. Arnie had taken me to Lutèce, another superb French restaurant in New York, and when I was ready to pay Kathy back the twelve hundred dollars she had lent me for key money on the apartment, I decided a great dinner at Lutèce would be the best way to thank her for the interest-free loan. So I made a reservation; you have to call a month ahead to get a table at eight o'clock, but it's fairly easy to get one at six, which is better for us during the week anyway. I told Kathy I had a double surprise for her and to meet me in the lobby of the Waldorf at five forty-five.

"A double surprise! At the Waldorf! Barbara, you have to give me just a few details so I know—"

I laughed. "No, no, not that, Kathy. Don't you ever think about anything else? This involves dinner, and it's not at the hotel; that's just the meeting place. So dress up nicely so they don't think you're one of those hotel hookers."

Kathy was there in the lobby right on time, bursting with anticipation and curiosity, and we walked the few blocks down Fiftieth Street to the restaurant. It was a lovely fall evening, one of those absolutely perfect days you get in New York in early October, and it made me feel so good I couldn't resist hamming it up a little. When we got to the restaurant, a subdued-looking townhouse with a very discreet sign, I stopped and stared at the building as if I was an architecture student.

"I wonder what this is, Kathy? It looks like a brownstone house, but—"

"This is Lutèce, Barbara. Haven't you ever heard—"

I maintained my deadpan perfectly, but she had already seen through me.

"Barbara! You're taking me here! Fantastic!" She gave me a big hug, and I pulled away, laughing, and said, "Come on now, we have to act ladylike."

We sat downstairs in the garden, a sunny, spacious, relaxing room that somehow seems wonderfully informal despite the classic table settings and captains in tuxedos and dressed-up people, and had a sumptuous meal of fresh turbot and roast pigeon and chocolate soufflés. Kathy said she guessed the second surprise would come later in the evening and begged for at least a hint about what it was.

"Kathy, I'd love to be cruel and keep you in suspense, but the second surprise is now. And it comes with my gratitude." I reached into my purse and got the check and handed it to her.

"Oh," she said, seeming a little startled. "The loan for the key money. You know, I'd almost forgotten all about it."

"That's because we're so stinking rich now. But thanks again, Kathy. I am grateful."

She toasted me with her coffee cup, and as I put mine down I glanced at my watch and saw it was seven fifty-five and remembered that we had to give the table up at eight, so I asked for the check. It was $168, and I reached into my purse and got two hundred-dollar bills and put them in the little leather folder the check comes in, with the ends sticking out so the waiter could see it was ready. I was trying to figure out the tips for the waiters and captain in my head when I realized there was a man coming up to our table, and I heard a voice say, "Hello, Barbara. How's the food here—any good?"

I looked up and it was Mr. McCorry, a vice-president at my company and my boss's boss. He was smiling at me, but he glanced quickly at the two hundreds sticking out of the little leather folder, and suddenly they seemed incriminating and accusatory, as if "Sin Money" was stamped in red on the edges.

"Oh, hello, Mr. McCorry. Oh, yes, it's wonderful, as always."

"Good!" he said, with a humorous smile. "Then I'll stay! I'm part of the second shift. Nice to see you."

"Nice to see you. 'Bye."

He walked to a table in the back and joined two men I didn't recognize. I left thirty dollars for the waiters and handed the captain ten dollars and we left.

"He seems like a nice guy," Kathy said when we got outside. "Why did you seem kind of rattled?"

"He's going to wonder how I can afford to eat at Lutèce. And of course like an idiot I had to say 'as always' and make myself sound like a regular there. I've only been once before; one of my customers took me."

"Oh, I don't think he'll give it a second thought. You came tonight as a special occasion, and a boyfriend takes you there once in a while. Barbara, you can't feel guilty and act guilty, because then your nervousness makes people wonder when they otherwise wouldn't. You know what I mean? The best way not to arouse any suspicion at all is just to act natural and confident. Now he might wonder why you seemed nervous, but otherwise he would have just thought you were taking a friend out for a special dinner on her birthday, or whatever."

"You're right. I've got to stop feeling paranoid. And I've got to learn to think before I open my mouth. Oh, well, it was worth going through it just to learn those lessons."

"Brazen your way through, that's the secret. And speaking of brazen, let's call Paul or Tony and see if we can't arrange to get ourselves some cognac and some dinner money."

I laughed; good old Kathy. "I'm with you!"

We called both, but neither was in, so we went to that nice kind of living-room bar in the Helmsley Palace, and Kathy insisted on treating me to the cognac. Then we went home, promising each other to give Tony or Paul a chance at a rain check.

There was one other scary close call besides the Plato's incident, but this one was really unavoidable and a long shot and had nothing to do with my feeling paranoid; by that time I had learned my lesson. I had made a date with Arnie to go to the theater on a Saturday night, and on Thursday Michael called and wanted to take me to a party on Saturday. I told him I had already made plans to have dinner with a girl friend, and he got annoyed.

"Barbara, you know Saturday is usually our night. Why do you go ahead and make other plans? This is going to be a great party, and I already told them you're coming with me."

"Michael, first of all, Saturday is not always our night. I can't leave every Saturday open on the chance that you'll call me, and then try to make plans at the last minute if you don't. And this is *Thursday*—you could have called me much earlier in the week. And finally, what gives you the right to tell these people I'm going to come when you hadn't even talked to me about it yet? Since when do you make all my decisions for me? And do you really expect me to cancel my plans with my girl friend and maybe leave her stranded just to please you?"

"Well, what do you expect me to do? Go by myself?"

"Michael, I don't really care what you do. Ask someone else—I don't mind. Or go by yourself; if it's such a great party, you'll have fun anyway. When did you get this invitation, by the way? Today?"

"Uh, no, it was Tuesday."

"Tuesday! And you're calling me now! And *you* talk to me about lack of consideration. Michael, have a great time at your party, and maybe I'll talk to you next week." And I hung up on him before he could say anything.

I was very proud of myself. Not only had I not acted nervous or evasive, but by being firm and confident and positive I had managed to turn the tables on him and make *him* feel guilty. So I felt I had nothing to worry about.

But as it turned out, my little ploy backfired and I had lots to worry about. During the first intermission at the theater, Arnie and I went out to the lobby to smoke. A friend of Michael's passed by with his girl friend. Like the saying goes, if I didn't have bad luck I wouldn't have any luck at all, and he saw me and waved. I nodded, and right away I

155

felt destroyed. He had seen me talking with Arnie, obviously we were together, and there was no way in hell I could get out of it now. Arnie saw what happened, and of course he noticed my depressed expression.

"What's the matter? Is that your boyfriend?"

"Almost as bad—it's a friend of my boyfriend. And sure as hell he's going to tell Michael he saw me here with a guy. And what makes it really bad is that Michael wanted me to go to a party with him tonight, and I told him I couldn't because I was having dinner with a girl friend. And we had an argument about it."

"He doesn't know what's really going on, does he?"

"No, but he's going to be really pissed."

"Can you find the friend and ask him not to say anything?"

"No, that would just make it worse. He's Michael's friend, and he's on Michael's side. He's met me a couple of times, but he doesn't really know me. Arnie, what am I going to do? How am I going to talk my way out of this?"

Arnie thought for a minute and said, "Tell him the girl friend canceled at the last minute because of some emergency—she got sick or something—and you tried to call Michael but couldn't reach him. And then this guy called you and invited you to the theater and you thought, it's either that or sit home, so you went."

"Not bad—not bad at all. I'll call a girl friend and have her back up the story, and it just might work. It's a good thing one of us has some brains."

Arnie laughed and said, "Let me know what happens."

When I got home that night, I called Kathy and asked her to support my story if Michael should check with her.

"Of course I'll do it, Barbara, but whatever you do, don't call Michael—wait for him to say something to you. There's just an outside chance that this other guy won't tell him."

"I doubt that, but I guess you're right. I'll just wait for Michael to call me and start bitching and moaning."

But Michael never said a word about it, and that just made it much worse, because I was saddled with the uncertainty of not knowing whether the friend hadn't told him or whether Michael knew but didn't want to bring it up. He might want to wait and see what happened, or he might be scared that bringing it out in the open would lead to a really big fight and he'd end up losing me, or he might just want to save it for future ammunition. Or he might have realized that for me the tension of worrying about it and waiting to see if he'd say something was much worse than any confrontation. He'd decide that putting me through that tension and worrying would be the best punishment. I was tempted to bring it up with him just to get it over with and end my agony, but I couldn't, because of the slim chance that the friend hadn't told Michael. It was heads I lose, tails I lose.

But it reminded me yet again of what a tremendous strain it can be to live this double life. It's especially a problem with friends. I'm reluctant to tell them because of the danger, but when I have to hide something from them I can't feel as close to them as I could if I told them everything. But I don't tell, because the risk is the overriding factor; all it takes is one unintentional chance remark, one tiny little slip, and I could end up losing my job and any chance of getting another one and being disowned by my parents. Not to mention the fact that this is after all illegal, and although I probably wouldn't end up in jail I sure don't want any brushes with the law and a record for the rest of my life.

So the only friends who know are Kathy and Eric. Kathy knows, naturally, because she's the one who got me started, and Eric because I feel I can trust him completely, and he doesn't know anyone who knows me except of course Jerry. Then there are boyfriends, but that's a whole other situation that I'll talk about in the next chapter.

I never suspected that a lot of problems with leading the double life would come from within the business itself, but they do. All my customers are always asking me to take care of this friend and that friend, but I just tell them the truth: I can only work so much—I only *want* to work so much—and if there are too many guys it just increases the risk, because not all these friends are really close friends, and the more guys who know you the greater the chance you'll run into someone who does business with your company or knows somebody who knows you. It's a slight chance, and the odds are against it, but it's there; I always think that the odds against running into a coworker at Plato's Retreat are probably something like a thousand to one, but it happened.

It also works in the other direction: often a customer wants to try a new girl. Paul is especially keen on this, and at one point he kept asking Kathy and me to set him up with another girl—"just for variety," he said, assuring us it didn't mean he would see us any less often. Kathy and I talked about it and decided we'd just tell Paul the truth: we didn't know any other part-timers, and we weren't about to go looking because that would put us at tremendous risk of being discovered. And we told him we could provide him with all the variety he wanted; aside from the far-out stuff like S&M, we would do anything he asked for—or just about. I say "we," but it was actually Kathy who told him; she and I decided that since she had known him longer she would make the best ambassadress. Paul understood and accepted our decision with very good grace.

But probably the worst problem I had from within the business came from the most unlikely source—Mitch. He was a very good student and progressed wonderfully, and after a few months of my expert teaching—she said modestly —he had become a skillful and sensitive lover without losing any of his basic sweetness. I kept hoping he would find a girl friend and start a really good relationship. But he was so hung up about his looks and so shy because of his lack of experience in approaching and courting women that he never really made the proper effort. Another reason, I think, was that I kept him so satisfied, he didn't feel any need to go after other women.

But the bad part of this was that he started to depend on me also to meet a lot of his emotional needs, and he got more and more smitten and infatuated with me. It had gone way beyond a strictly business relationship right from the start, and I liked that, because I didn't want any strictly business clients, but after a few months it began to get out of hand.

The first week in December, after we had known each other for about six months, I went to Mitch's apartment for a date and saw a beautifully gift-wrapped box on the couch, obviously a Christmas present, looking very festive in its gold wrapping paper and big red ribbon.

"Aha," I said, "I see you've already started your Christmas shopping. I do most of mine at the last minute, and I hate people like you who get it done in good time. But what is it, and who is it for?"

"Barbara, you shouldn't ask what it is—and the fact that you shouldn't ask is the only hint I'm going to give you about who the lucky recipient is."

"It's for—for me? Oh, Mitch, you don't have to do that—you're so sweet."

He grinned at me. "Not sweet at all. I'm going to be a real meanie and put a big 'Do Not Open Until Christmas' sign on it!"

"And make me die of curiosity for *weeks?* Mitch, please! Anything but that! Besides, what if it's perishable—or something that should be kept lying on its side?"

"Don't try that on me, Ignoto. No hints. If you treat me *really* nice, I might let you open it tonight."

I had one of my brilliant sudden inspirations. I stripped off my dress and went over to the package and tucked the end of the ribbon into the top of my panties. I smiled at

Mitch teasingly and said, "Is it okay if I just wear the ribbon?"

Mitch loved it. He started laughing and clapping his hands like a spectator at a burlesque show. "Yes, yes! You may wear *just* the ribbon!"

I slid my panties down seductively then undid the ribbon and drew it back and forth across my pussy; it felt a little rough but very erotic, and I was already starting to get wet. Mitch was taking off his clothes, watching me, and I brought the ribbon up and pulled it back and forth across my breasts. Mitch sat back, naked and playing with his hard-on, and said, "I'm going to let you open it now, but only for a selfish reason—I want to see you model it. It'll look and feel fantastic on you when you're nude."

"Aha! I know—it's a negligee. Or a shortie nightgown. I should have known you'd get me something like that, you horny bastard."

Mitch didn't say a word but just sat there grinning at me with a mixture of joy and desire. I tore off the wrapping, letting the ribbon fall to the floor, lifted off the top of the box, and then gasped with surprise.

Nestled in the box, beautifully folded, its deep, rich burnished brown color set off by white tissue paper, was a mink coat.

I froze for a moment and just stood there looking at it. Then I turned and looked at Mitch; he was beaming with delight.

"Mitch—oh, Mitch—you shouldn't have done this. I can't take this—as a Christmas present. It's just too much."

"Well, okay, Barbara, if you won't accept it as a Christmas gift, make it an engagement present." He had tried to say it casually, as a witty throwaway line, but his voice broke on the word "engagement."

Speechless for a moment, I looked into his face, into his eyes; his smile had faded, and he looked back at me with tenderness and pleading.

"Oh, Mitch, Mitch, I can't—you mustn't—" I started crying and couldn't say any more. Mitch stood up uncertainly, unsure of what to do or say, and I fell against him and wrapped my arms around him, and he held me gently while I cried.

After a minute or so I got myself under control. I moved away from him a little and looked up into his face.

"Mitch, you're sweet. Too sweet. And I'm so fond of you —too fond of you for my own good—or yours. This is something that just can't be. You know that. You must realize that." I put my right hand very gently on his cheek and caressed him with my fingers. "I'm so sorry. I really am. I like you tremendously. But—you know. I just can't. We can't."

He looked into my eyes, not saying anything, then slowly took my hand from his cheek and drew it to his mouth and softly kissed my fingertips. "I need to sit down," he said, and we moved back and sat on one corner of the couch. The box lay crookedly in the other corner, the coat facing up into the room like a silent bystander, listening, and suddenly there flashed in my mind's eye an image of the animal it had been, running in the woods and stepping into the quick metal arm of the trap.

Mitch looked very sad. "I guess you're right. I guess, Barbara, this is just another one of the stupid things I do. But I feel so close to you, you know—closer than I do to anyone. When you're not around, I miss you. In the back of my mind I knew this was a crazy thing, a long shot, but—ah, what's the use." He was silent for a moment, then said, "But do take the coat anyway." He smiled weakly. "As a Christmas present."

"But, Mitch, don't you see, that's just it—that's just why I can't take it as a Christmas gift, for the same reason I can't accept it as an engagement present. I'm leading two lives, and this isn't my real life. If I took the coat, how would I explain it? Who gave it to me? Or how did I get the money to buy it for myself? Don't you see? I have to keep this life totally separate from my real life. Well, this life is real too, but I mean from my main life or my private life or whatever you want to call it. I can't let one intrude on the other. The part-time life intrudes emotionally, but I can't help that, I just have to deal with it as best I can. I have lots of problems in my private life right now with boyfriends and potential boyfriends, and I haven't any idea what the solution is. But of course this certainly isn't it. I don't want to hurt you, because I do like you a lot, but that's exactly why I want you to understand this. Because to hide this, this having to lead a double life, or pretend it doesn't affect our relationship would really be cruel."

Mitch nodded. "I see. I do understand. So." He sighed. "So I guess the best thing is just to forget about all this and not mention it again and try to go on like we have been."

"You're right. That is the best way. But I want you to know how much I do appreciate the gift even though I can't take it. I hate to say it's the thought that counts, because that sounds so stupid and such a cliché, but that's it, isn't it? —it *is* the thought that really shows how you feel."

Mitch looked at me and gave me a sweet, sad smile, and then that irrepressible touch of mischief came out, and I knew he was going to be all right. "I'll remember that," he said, "when all you get me for Christmas is a *Penthouse* calendar."

I laughed and said, "Just you wait and see!" and suddenly I felt a tremendous surge of tenderness and affection for him. I reached down for his cock, limp now, and cradled his cock and balls in my hand and gave him a deep kiss. He gently teased my tongue with his, then kissed me harder, and I felt his cock grow hard in my hand. All at once I wanted him very much, and quickly, and I felt no need nor patience for preliminaries. I knelt down in front of him and sucked him fast and intensely for a few moments and then reached up for him and pulled him down on top of me on the carpet. He entered me slowly, and we began a long, delicious, lingering lovemaking that made us bask in a glow of devotion and sentiment. Even though we felt an intense passion and need for each other, it was completely free of any sense of urgency or conquest; there was gentleness and fragile sweetness and a kind of delicacy that made it seem as if we had all the time in the world. The room seemed to tilt slowly back and forth, and then it fell away and I felt as if we were floating up into space, rising higher and higher, spinning toward the sun, then a great warmth, and his body and mine coming together in a burst of joy and incredible release, seeming to last forever.

Then time and space returned, and we were lying back on the carpet. We turned our heads and looked into each other's eyes and smiled; there was no need to say anything. We lay there for a minute, not wanting to let go of the moment. Then I kissed him lightly and whispered, "Good night," and he smiled and said softly, "Sweet dreams," and I got dressed quickly and let myself out. It wasn't until I got home that I realized that this was the first time I had ever seen a customer without taking or wanting money.

The next day on my lunch hour I went over to Madison Avenue and ordered some fine stationery for Mitch and made them promise it would be ready in a week. Then I bought the best fountain pen I could find. A week later I picked up the stationery and bought all my Christmas cards, giftwrap, and some big red ribbon, and one copy each of *The Village Voice, New York* magazine, and *The New York Review of Books.* That night at home I carefully cut the personal ads out of each publication, folded them neatly, and wrapped them up in a nice package with the stationery and the fountain pen. I tied a red ribbon around the package, made a nice big bow, and then went on to put together my other Christmas presents.

VI.   Private Loves

What I told Mitch about having problems with my boy-friend situation was only too true. The incident with Mi-chael over my not going to that Saturday night party was just one argument among many.

Even before the party, Michael had already begun to sus-pect that I might be cheating on him, because I was getting so much more demanding sexually and showed so much abandon in bed. He didn't say anything directly, but he started to question me about what I was doing and where I was going, to the point where it became obvious that he thought I was stepping out for some strange stuff.

The funny thing, of course, was that in a literal sense I was being totally faithful to him. I wasn't sleeping with or even seeing anyone else on a private basis; the only other guys I went with were my customers. I was tremendously tempted by Steven, but because I really did like Michael and didn't want to two-time him, I restricted myself to calling Steven once in a while and telling him that if he could just be patient awhile longer, then someday we could get together. And he was incredibly patient; he'd joked about being too old when I finally got around to him but said that by then I'd make him feel young again and that I was worth waiting for.

My mother invited Michael over for Thanksgiving dinner, and we had such a warm and wonderful time that for a few hours I deceived myself into thinking that we could somehow work things out. My mother liked Michael a lot and couldn't understand why I wasn't eager to marry him. I could hardly tell her that I had started to find him very dull sexually, so I just explained that I wasn't ready to marry anyone yet, that I thought it could wait a few years—which was how I really did feel.

Michael and I left my parents' place at about nine o'clock Thanksgiving night, feeling very mellow and happy. He had called a cab for us, and on the way back to Manhattan we necked, just like old times. By the time we got to his place we had worked ourselves into quite a state. We got undressed quickly, and Michael started the same old routine of caressing my tits and then moving around for a sixty-nine.

"Let's do each other separately this time," I said, gently pushing his ass away from me. He gave a little grunt and moved his head toward my pussy, but I said seductively, "Start up here first—suck my tits. Give me a real tongue bath."

"I'm not a *cat,*" he said with a trace of disgust, and licked perfunctorily at one nipple for a few seconds, then moved down and started sucking my pussy in his usual inexpert, mediocre way. I felt very sad and frustrated and I thought, *Here's this guy that I really like as a person, who's generous and nice, and here he is in bed as my real lover, no money involved, pure romance, and he's not* one-tenth *as good as those guys who pay me. And if I try to show him or ask for something, he makes a stupid crack like that. Maybe actions speak louder than words,* and I pulled away from him and lifted my ass off the bed and up in the air a little, hoping he'd get the idea and start rimming me, but he just eased me back down onto the bed and started licking my cunt again. I was getting more and more turned off, and my pussy was still dry, and I thought, *Surely he'll notice that, but what will he do about it—will he ask me about it?* But either he didn't notice or he pretended he didn't, and after a while he stopped sucking me and lay back on the bed so I could go down on him.

But I didn't. I just lay there awhile, then heaved myself up with obvious reluctance, and he said, "What's the matter?"

How perceptive, I thought; *how sensitive.*

"Can't you tell?"

"No."

I thought, *The hell with it, what's the use,* and started sucking his cock. My mind was a million miles away while I was doing it; I told myself I had to face the fact that I had outgrown Michael sexually and he would probably never catch up. But then I realized that even though I was in no mood for a regular fuck, I wouldn't mind at all getting screwed in the ass again, and that doing it might turn Michael on enough and surprise him enough so we could at least talk about opening up our sex life.

I sucked him some more until he was really hot and ready, then I lifted my head and looked at him and said very seductively, "Michael, I've got a great surprise for you. I'm going to let you fuck me in the ass."

"Oh, come on, Barbara, I don't do that. That's for queers."

I thought, *Oh, shit, let's get this over with,* and started sucking him again, quickly and intensely to make him come as soon as possible, and in a few seconds it was over.

I got up and went to the bathroom and spat out his come. I felt drained and exhausted, and I just wanted to get out of there as fast as possible. I was in no mood for any kind of confrontation. He seemed threatened by the new, sexually demanding Barbara, but I didn't know what to do about it, and at that point I didn't really care.

I went back in the bedroom and he was still lying on the bed, looking ready to fall asleep at any second. He's fairly good-looking, with nice brown curly hair and fine facial features and just the beginnings of a pot belly, but at that moment he seemed faintly repulsive to me.

"Are you all right?" he asked. "You seem kind of out of sorts tonight."

"I'm just tired," I said, picking up my clothes and starting to put them on. "Too much food and too long a day. You look kind of sleepy yourself, so I'll just split and go home and hit the sack."

"Okay. Happy Thanksgiving."

"Happy Thanksgiving, Michael. And sweet dreams. Goodnight."

On the way home in the cab, I was fighting with myself. My brain said, *This is over, put an end to it cleanly and quickly, call Steven tomorrow—he's there just waiting for you.* But my heart said, *Give Michael one more chance; you've been with him over a year and had good times; you basically like him a lot, at least outside the bedroom; you might be able to awaken him sexually if you can just figure out the right way, so he doesn't feel threatened.* By the time I got home I had myself thoroughly confused, and, as usual when I needed help and advice, I decided to turn to Kathy.

We met for dinner on Sunday at our old standby in Little Italy. I thought about what a sense of security it gave me to have those old familiar things always ready for me to return to—the restaurant, Kathy, my parents and their home at Thanksgiving—and I realized that Michael was on the list, and that was one reason I was reluctant to dump him. I mentioned that to Kathy after I had told her about the troubled romance and the Thanksgiving night disaster.

She nodded, chewing thoughtfully on the last piece of her lobster fra diavolo, then she put her knife and fork decisively across her plate and said, "I've got an idea. He doesn't know about the part-time thing, does he?"

"No. I'd like to tell him, because I'd feel closer to him, but I'm afraid to because he can be so uptight. He'd probably have me arrested."

"Well, maybe, but it might also turn him on so much that

167

it would give you a chance to draw him out sexually. Some of my boyfriends have gotten terrifically excited by it. Tell him you know a girl who's doing this—without mentioning me, naturally—and just see what his reaction is. If he's stimulated, you can take it from there, and if he isn't, no harm done."

"That's a good plan. But if he's appalled at the idea, where do I go from there?"

"Why not just drop him? I know it's going to leave you feeling adrift and alone for a while, but you won't have any trouble finding someone new."

I smiled. "Actually, I've already got a couple of hot prospects." And I told her about Steven and about Joe, the actor who drove a taxi part-time.

"Barbara, if you've got your choice of two good guys, you should jump at the chance to get away from Michael. I know you like him and all that, but if you're not *happy* with him anymore, what's the point? It's fine to be sentimental, but if you end up being a masochist and torturing yourself— I don't know, you're usually so level-headed, I really don't understand why you're letting this drag out."

"I don't either, I guess. But I'll give it this one last shot, and if that doesn't work out, then it's time to end the affair."

Kathy spooned up the last of her zabaglione, tapped the plate softly with her spoon, and said, "All good things have to end sometime."

I called Michael that night and told him I thought we needed to have a long talk; he heartily agreed, and we made a date for Maxwell's Plum on Monday.

The meal started out well; we had a good table in the back room, and Michael had made good progress on a leasing deal that day and was in a good mood. He also seemed kind of solicitous and conciliatory, as if he had an inkling that this might be the last chance to straighten out our relationship. We ordered Maxwell's excellent black bean soup, thick and grainy and winy, and the rack of lamb with vegetables, and a bottle of Montrose. I wanted to bring up the news about the part-time acquaintance in a natural way, so I asked him if it was true that hookers sometimes came to the bar at Maxwell's late at night.

"Oh, no, I think that's just a rumor, probably started by some rival restaurant. This place wouldn't tolerate them."

"I know a girl who does that part-time—she turns three or four tricks a week to earn extra money."

"That's terrible. The whole thing is so sordid and tacky—and dangerous. I hope you can talk her out of it."

"Well, I don't know. Sometimes people get into a bad bag but they don't really want to hear about it. You'd like to offer them advice, but it's hard to get them to listen."

"Barbara, I guess that's a hint, and I'll take it. You and I have hit some rocky road, but I think you're the one who doesn't want to listen."

"Michael, have you ever asked yourself why we're not getting along like we used to?"

"No, I haven't, because I already know."

"Well, great, but if you know, why don't you do something about it?"

"Why don't *I* do something about it? I'm not the one who's playing around."

"What do you mean?"

"Barbara, come off it. I know all about you, and you know it."

"Oh, Michael, if you only realized how little you really know about me."

"You gave me that bullshit about you couldn't go to that party because you were going to see your girl friend and then you went to the theater with that guy. Lenny saw you, and you know he did, so what's the big innocent act? Do you think I'm an idiot?"

"I went to the theater because my girl friend got sick and

I couldn't reach you and then this guy invited me, so I went instead of sitting home. It's no big deal."

"And the apartment? You thought you were being so clever not telling me how much it costs, but it's obvious you can't afford it on your salary, and it's equally obvious this guy is helping you pay your rent."

"Michael, calm down. You're getting angry over something that isn't even true. You've got these two pieces of 'evidence,' and neither one of them means anything."

"How about the biggest piece of evidence, Barbara? How come you've started to act like a whore in bed?"

"Like a what?"

"You heard what I said."

"Michael, you owe me an apology for that. Now."

"You owe *me* an apology. And you know something, if I got it I'd probably forgive you, or we could at least really talk about this. If you came to me and said, 'I had a fling with this other guy and I got carried away and did whatever he wanted and he helped me with my rent but now I realize it was a mistake and I'm sorry and I hope you can forgive me,' then all right. Okay. But there's no trust, nothing. I always liked you because you were open and didn't play games, but now it's just the opposite—it's nothing but secrecy and dirty games."

He threw down his fork, disgusted, then slumped back and looked away from me, staring straight ahead.

I couldn't say anything. I took a long drink of the wine and put the glass down slowly and stared into it, as if some kind of answer were hidden in that beautiful red liquid. I felt weird—very, very sad but also relieved that it was finally over. And it was overwhelmingly clear that it was, past the point of no return, over.

"Michael." I reached over and put my hand on his on the table and looked into his face. "I met you in this restaurant, and I guess it's here that I leave you. That we leave each other." The anger had gone from his face and he looked puzzled and hurt and sad. "It's been—fun. Most of it. I hope you have a wonderful and very happy life." I leaned over and gave him a last kiss then quickly grabbed my bag and slid out from the table and got up and stood facing him for a moment. He looked at me and tried to smile but it was only a tense tightening of the lips. "Good-bye, Barbara." He looked unbearably sad.

I turned away and walked toward the door, and the tears started to come before I got to the maître d's stand. He looked at me with concern, and I realized that he recognized me from the evening with Jerry and Eric. He took my elbow gently and helped me down the stairs from the back room and said, "Goodnight," seriously and sympathetically. I made my way out to the street and opened the door of the first cab on line and got in.

I took out a handkerchief and dabbed at my eyes as we headed up First Avenue. I wondered if the breakup would have happened if I hadn't started my other life, and I reflected that it would have been inevitable anyway. I wouldn't have gone with Michael forever. I would have become bored with him even if I hadn't been so sexually awakened by being a part-timer. That had just made the split happen sooner. It wasn't all for the best—because now there was no chance that we could at least remain friends—but at least it was over. It left a sadness, but I didn't want to let the sadness take hold of me. I didn't want to think about it anymore. I wanted to think about Steven.

I called Steven when I got home, half-expecting to get his answering machine, but he was there.

"Hi. It's Barbara."

"Barbara! How great to hear from you. I hope this isn't going to be another 'Please be patient.'"

"No, that's all over now—you've already shown more patience than ten saints. I'd love to see you, and I thought we could have dinner some night this week."

"Sure. Actually, I was just getting ready to go out for a bite now, if you want to join me tonight."

"I'm really not quite in the mood. I just now broke up with my boyfriend."

"Oh. I see. Well, tomorrow is no good for me, but how about Wednesday?"

"Wednesday is great, if we can make it on the early side. I'm a nine-to-fiver, I'm afraid, and I have to get up early."

"Six o'clock is fine. Now what is your favorite restaurant? Just name it and you got it."

I laughed. I didn't want to say that my absolute favorite was La Grenouille because I didn't know whether he could spend that much, and even if he could it would make me seem kind of greedy. I wanted to let him know what I liked but still leave the choice in his hands, so I said, "I haven't been to a good Northern Italian place in a long time, so if there's one you really like, let's do that."

"Il Valletto—best Italian food in town. Sixty-first just west of Lex. Barbara, I can't wait. I know that sounds funny after I've waited all these months, but I am so looking forward to seeing you. Have a light lunch."

"I always do—it's good for the figure. See you Wednesday. 'Bye."

Il Valletto turned out to be big and plush and bright and cheerful and two hundred percent Italian. Steven hadn't arrived yet, and the restaurant was almost empty, and I was cosseted and charmed and treated with that special Italian warmth by the maître d'hotel and the captain and waiters. And after I spoke a few words of Italian, they *really* made me feel like a queen. I tried to order a glass of white wine, but the captain wouldn't hear of it. "Ah, *no,* Signorina, I am sure Mr. Garson will want to celebrate his good fortune with some champagne!"

Steven came in just then, looking even more attractive than I remembered him, with that lock of blond hair falling over his forehead and those absolutely unbelievable gray-blue eyes, smoky and warm, as if they contained an intense inner fire despite his relaxed, easy manner. He was wearing a burgundy-colored blazer and a deep-blue tie and looked casual and elegant.

He grinned and said to the captain with mock anger, "Tony! Don't fall in love with my date so fast, please. Give me a chance, will you?"

Tony pulled out the table for Steven and gave an eloquent shrug. "If you insist, Signore Garson. Perhaps if I bring you a bottle of Krug from my hidden stock you might forgive me?"

"Perhaps," Steven said deliberately, and then gave me that stunning sunrise smile and leaned over and kissed me full on the lips. Not what you'd ordinarily do at the beginning of a first date, but this guy could make anything seem natural—and compelling. I put my hand on his leg and jabbed my tongue in and out of his mouth and sucked his tongue, and that was it. Those few moments immediately swept away all the questions and game-playing and every other barrier. I'd never been so infatuated with anyone in my whole life.

"Forgive my presumption," he said, adding with perfect timing, "I should have asked you first whether you like champagne."

I laughed and took my hand off his leg. "I'll forgive all your presumptions, Steven—I'll forgive you anything. And I love champagne."

The Krug was even richer and more wonderful than Taittinger. Steven said the trenette al pesto was superb there and asked Tony if it was too late in the year for pesto sauce.

"Ah, no, Signore Garson, we have it, but we have fresh white truffles tonight, and I don't think those would be good with pesto. But perhaps one order of trenette al pesto and one order of fettuccine Alfredo with truffles, and you and the lady can share."

173

"Perfect. And seafood salads to start, and one order of sautéed zucchini, and a bottle of Orvieto?"

"Benissimo!"

"Steven, you're the man of my dreams. Will you marry me?"

He laughed delightedly. "I can't. I'd say yes in a second, but I can't, because I travel so much."

"For the photography? What kind do you do?"

"Anything and everything. Fashion, corporate, PR, some news assignments. Whatever's lucrative enough to support my extravagant lifestyle."

"I'll quit my job and travel with you."

"You're a teacher?"

"No, just a secretary. But you made a good guess. I've toyed with the idea of becoming a teacher."

"It'd be worth it just to have the summer off. You could travel with me then."

"I've never been anywhere, hardly to New Jersey, and I want to hear all about your trips."

Steven obliged, and it was fascinating and romantic: London, Paris, the Caribbean, Bangkok. The food was excellent; we shared a wonderful almond cake for dessert, and of course there was *real* espresso. I decided I'd have to come to Il Valletto with Kathy and get us out of our tomato-sauce rut.

Steven asked me what I'd like to do after dinner, and I smiled and said, "A long, slow walk to your place—unless you live in Brooklyn Heights."

"No, no—Seventy-ninth and Park."

"Perfect—sixteen blocks. Just perfect." I couldn't resist stroking the back of his neck. "Everything about you is perfect." That thousand-watt smile again, and we stepped out into the evening.

We had hardly gotten through his door before we were wrapped in a passionate embrace. He reached behind me and unzipped my dress and stroked my back with his strong hand, and I ground myself against his hard-on. Then we pulled away from each other and practically ran into the bedroom. Steven kicked off his shoes and threw his blazer onto a chair and started to take off his tie, but I said, "Wait —let me undress you."

I slid my dress off my shoulders and pulled it down so he could see my breasts, then took off his tie and unbuttoned his shirt, helping him off with it. His chest was beautiful, broad and solidly muscled and covered with fine blond hairs. I licked his nipples and then all over his whole chest, unzipping his fly in the meantime and putting my hand inside his shorts to stroke his hard cock. I went back to his nipples and sucked them, then ran my tongue up his chest and licked his armpit. Steven was moaning with pleasure and his cock was throbbing in my hand. I gave his cock one last caress and unbuckled his belt and undid his pants, moving around to suck the other armpit. His cock was so big and hard, I had trouble getting his pants down, but I got them off and then the shorts and knelt before him and licked his balls and up and down the length of his cock. Then I turned him around so he could lie face down across the bed, and I stuck my tongue in his ass. I pulled his socks off and massaged his feet while I really got into sucking his ass, driving him wild. "Oooh, Barbara, that's so beautiful . . . that's wonderful . . . oh, God."

When I finally stopped, I took my dress off all the way and lay back on the bed. Steven slipped my panties down and sucked my clit and pussy slowly and expertly, reaching up to caress my breasts at the same time, stroking and squeezing my nipples and making them get harder and harder. I started coming in a great wonderful wave, and when it subsided I tried to push him away, but he kept at it and those moments of excruciating sensitivity passed and I came again. Steven moved up and sucked my nipples deliciously and then entered me slowly. I had never felt so wet and tight and ready for anyone, and Steven was a superb lover, moving slowly and deeply and filling me up completely with that beautiful big cock. He lasted a long time, and I marveled at his control. I started coming again long before he did, and then he started moving faster and faster, but still with perfect supple control, not frantic, and I put my legs inside his and he wrapped me tightly and I could feel him coming, feel every spasm of his cock, and I came again and again, with him.

He pulled out slowly and gave me a tender kiss. I said, "Wow. Wow. You're the best. How can you last so long?" He gave me a sexy smile and said, "Make love every day."

Steven wasn't just kidding. We talked for a while, then he rimmed me and went down on me again and we did a sixty-nine and finished that way. Twice in one night was usually his limit, but he could do that day after day, and it was the beginning of a wild, marvelous, dizzyingly erotic love affair.

For the first couple of months, I was seeing Steven so often, three and four times a week when he was in town, that I had to cut the number of customers I was seeing down to two or three during those weeks. Between Steven and the customers, I got up to an exquisitely high sexual pitch, and the days seemed to float by in a haze of pleasure. Steven and I got into a lot of threesomes with friends of his, male and female, and we did everything. I liked to suck one guy while the other guy fucked me or eat out the girl while Steven screwed me, and to get screwed in the pussy and ass at the same time, and all of us loved to get rimmed and sucked at the same time. One of Steven's girl friends was especially turned on by rimming him while he fucked me and then sucking his come out of my ass or pussy. And after Steven had come the first time, he liked to watch me and another girl give each other tongue baths. Steven was always eager to do some complete swapping too, but I told him I didn't want to because then I might not make it with him and I'd feel like I belonged to the other guy. With the threesomes it was always clear, no matter what we did, that Steven and I were together.

It didn't take me long to decide that I wanted to tell Steven about my second job; if anyone could handle it, he could. When I told him I knew a girl who was a part-time call girl, he was fascinated and wanted to know all about it. And the next time Steven and I made love by ourselves, I told him the girl wanted me to try it with one of her customers.

"Oh, great. Do it, Barbara. Do you want to?"

"Sure. She says he's a nice guy, and I'd like to try it."

"What does he like?"

"She didn't say, but I'd do just about anything for him, you know."

"Oh, yeah, do it, and I want to hear all about it, all the juicy details."

We had already made love twice, but Steven had gotten hard as a rock again just thinking about my "first" trick. I stroked his cock and then went down on him and sucked him off very slowly while he told me all the things he wanted me to do for the customer—suck his nipples and his ass and balls and let him fuck me in the ass. Since Steven had already come twice, I thought he was going to last forever, but he got himself so hot talking that he shot in my mouth after what seemed like just a few seconds.

I started telling Steven about my paid adventures, and he got tremendously excited hearing about them, especially about the sessions with Eric and Paul. I suggested that we party with Eric, but Steven said that although he loved hearing about it, the gay trip just wasn't his thing.

Our problems began when Steven had to start traveling an awful lot. He always wanted me to come with him, but I told him that although I'd like nothing better, I just couldn't take the time off from work.

Then one night in February we were lying in bed after

making love, and he told me he was going to Martinique for five days and urged me to come along.

"It's the perfect time now, Barbara—it's warm and sunny there, and they have some great French food, and of course it's all on me. Take a week of your vacation."

"God, Steven, you know I'd love to, but I just can't. I can't get a week on such short notice. And I want to go to Italy and France in September, so I need the whole four weeks I've got coming for that trip."

"Barbara, why don't you quit your job? Then you can travel with me whenever you want—your time will be your own."

"Quit my job? How will I support myself?"

"You know—just do the call-girl thing full-time. You'll make enough so you can take two weeks off with no sweat."

"Oh, no, I'm not going to go full-time. I *never* want to do that. Then you really become a whore, and you lose your real life and your cover story with everyone who knows you —you lose everything, and you can never get it back. Uh-unh. Never."

"But at least you'll have your freedom—you can live like you want and do what you want. Do you want to be a secretary all your life?"

"Maybe I don't, but that's not the point. I don't want to screw myself up so I can't do anything else, and I don't want to do it full-time. Period."

"Barbara, you're being silly. You're passing up all sorts of great experiences so you can sit in an office all day five days a week and take dictation and type. You can always go back to that if you want."

I was getting really angry. "Steven, don't say it's silly. It's my decision. I told you about three times already, goddammit, *I don't want to be a full-time call girl.* Now let's drop it, once and for all."

But now he was getting pissed too. "Barbara, you're getting to be a pain. Susan or Jessica would love to go with me, they practically beg me to come along sometimes, and I always tell them no until I ask you because I'd rather go with you. I give you first chance, and you don't appreciate it. You won't even try to get one week off."

I was furious. I'd never before admitted to myself that I was jealous of his other women, but his using them against me really infuriated me.

"So go with them, goddammit! I don't give a shit!" I jumped out of bed and started to get dressed. "If you can't understand that I want to but I just can't, then the hell with you!" I stormed out of his apartment before he could say anything, slamming the door behind me.

That little scene ended our affair. He didn't send me a card from the trip as he usually did, and he didn't call when he got back. I was tempted to call him, but I was still so angry about his not understanding that I decided to just try to forget about him for a while and see what would happen.

That started me on a period of one disappointing and relatively brief romance after another. I'm not happy if I don't have anyone at all—to me, no relationship is like no life—and I guess I got so anxious just to have a lover that I didn't take enough time or care to find the right guys.

The first thing I did was call Joe, the actor. He was surprised to hear from me, because it had been so long since we'd met in his cab that he thought I'd forgotten all about him. He took me to dinner at Joe Allen's, an actors' hangout on the West Side where the food is cheap and okay, and we hit it off fairly well. He was interesting and had a great sense of humor, and he was pretty good in bed; not as exciting as Steven, but light years better than Michael. I ran through what had become my standard routine about telling my secret: first mentioning the girl friend to test the guy's reaction, then the proposal that I try it with one of her customers. Joe was turned on by the idea, just like Steven, and got just as excited hearing all the juicy details.

We got along fine for a few months, but the problem with Joe was that he was poor. I guess I'd gotten spoiled by being with all those wealthy guys, but Joe never seemed to have any money, and we started to fight about going Dutch and splitting dinner checks. When he tried to borrow two hundred dollars from me, that was the last straw.

I started hanging out in singles' bars again, and I met Marty, a stockbroker who seemed very nice and shared my preoccupation with good food. But he turned out to be kind of another Michael; he seemed threatened by my being sexually demanding and wild, and when I told him about the part-timer girl friend, he was so appalled that I said I had just been kidding. We struggled along for about seven weeks, with me trying to loosen him up and turn him on, but I didn't get anywhere, and I thought, *I don't need this all over again.*

Number three on this sad list was Matthew, a college professor of English who picked me up at Sam Goody's with such deftness and charm that I almost forgot the records I had come to buy. We were very, very different, but physically we were very attracted, and somehow our different interests and outlooks on life made us seem more fascinating to each other and intensified the attraction. It was summer, and Matthew had a big apartment on Riverside Drive, so we'd often spend weekend days sunbathing in the park, then go to his apartment and make love before going out to dinner. He was a demanding lover in a kind of pedantic way— "Do this; no, over there"; "Faster"; "Don't be so gentle!"— that I liked; it was unusual and exciting in an offbeat way. And he was very skilled and willing to experiment. He was intrigued when I told him about the part-timer girl friend; he wanted to know all about her background and how she lived and what she spent her money on. Then I told him about myself, and that turned out to be a mistake. He was as excited by it as Steven and Joe, but it turned him into an amateur shrink with me. He had to know all about my motivations and how it affected me emotionally and what kind of conflicts I had and so on and on and on. I found it only mildly annoying until one day while we were sunbathing he said, "You know, the worst thing about it is that it makes you even more materialistic than you already are."

"Materialistic? What do you mean?"

"Oh, you know, you define your life too much in terms of how much money you have, and your possessions, and being able to take cabs all the time and go to good restaurants, and not enough in terms of emotional values—intellectual and spiritual values."

"Well, I don't think one means you can't have the other. You can like to live well and still be a good person. Everyone likes to live well—you like to, and you do."

"Yes, but I don't let it dominate my life and form my values and my outlook."

"That's because you're well off to start with. Calling people materialistic—that's always done by people who have the material things and don't have the faintest idea what it's like to be without them."

He was silent for a minute then said, "You know, we're so very different."

"We sure are. We certainly are."

"It's kind of miraculous we've stayed together as long as we have."

I smiled at him fondly but with a twinge of sadness. His was a nice change, in a way, from the blunt approach of the other men I knew.

"It's been a wonderful summer, Matthew—a wonderful summer romance."

It was his turn to smile sadly. "Summer is almost over. Next week is Labor Day. A summer romance is a summer romance, isn't it?"

"What's that song?" And I sang it softly:

Let's call it a day,
The civilized way. . . .

Matthew reached over and took my hand. *"Can* we do it the civilized way, Barbara? Can we still be friends?"

I squeezed his hand in mind and said, "Please. Let's. Let's still be friends. Even if we just meet once every July for dinner."

"I'd like that. And in the meantime, I wish you the best."

I leaned over and kissed him, and the fondness I felt for him and my gratitude for the gentleness of our split flickered into desire, and I said, "Matthew, I can think of a wonderful way to say good-bye."

He opened his mouth and kissed me deeply, and we went to his apartment and made love for the last time in the heat of the late afternoon, with the breeze coming in off the river and the faint happy sounds of weekending New Yorkers wafting up from the park. This last time there were no words, but there was a wonderful affection and tenderness. Then I got my stuff together and there was a final embrace and kiss and promises to stay in touch.

I walked up the hot and sunny street to Broadway and got a cab. I guess I had known from the beginning that it had to end, because we were so different, but I still felt sad, especially because he was so decent and it had ended in such a nice way without yelling and fighting and bitterness. But I reflected that it had been the third false start in a row, and I felt weary to the bottom of my soul and terribly lonely. I needed to talk to someone. I called Kathy, but she wasn't home. But Eric was, thank God, and we went to dinner at Raoul's. After I had poured out my troubles to him and we talked and had a good meal, my mood improved a little, but I still felt that I needed someone—a relationship. I went home again, fervently wishing that Eric weren't gay.

September came, and the fall, my favorite season in New York, when the weather is perfect and the restaurants are reopening after summer vacation and the theater and jazz clubs are starting up full blast again. It seems like a time of renewal and rebirth, a chance to start again, especially in love, and it got so that I wanted Steven so badly I was tempted to call him and ask if we could get back together again.

I had gotten a passport and scheduled my vacation starting the third week in September, but I felt so lonely and blue that I kind of lost my desire to go to Italy and France. I could afford it now, but I didn't want to travel by myself, and I couldn't work up enough ambition to start making plans.

Then one night when I got home there was a message on my machine. "Barbara—it's Steven. Please call me. Remember that to err is human, to forgive, *divine*. Be divine." I smiled; he was so wonderful, and I was so delighted he had called. I was dialing even before the tape finished rewinding.

"Steven, how are you!? What's happening? I'm going to be, as I always am, divine."

He laughed. "Great! I owe you an apology—I shouldn't have been so insistent about your going full-time, and I do understand how you feel about it. Listen, I'm going to Paris for a few weeks for some fashion shooting, and I remember your saying you were going to take your vacation around this time, so I was hoping you'd like to come along with me. I know you wanted to go to Italy too, but you can do Italy next year and—"

I was so excited I interrupted him. "Steven! Yes! Yes! I'd love to! God, it sounds fantastic!"

It turned out to be better than fantastic. I fell madly in love with Paris from the moment the cab from the airport got to the city and turned onto a wide boulevard lined with townhouses whose stone fronts had a golden glow in the morning sunlight. There were trees and flowers and elegant little stores and cafés, and all the people looked chic and stylish. And the light! It was different in Paris, with a softness and clarity and a kind of glow that made this lovely city even more beautiful.

Steven had gotten me a room at the Plaza-Athenée, a dazzlingly beautiful and luxurious hotel with incredible service. And he had told me to get some sleep during the day so I wouldn't be wiped out by jet lag and to meet him for dinner at Taillevent at eight o'clock. I left a call for five P.M., unpacked, took a shower, and crawled into that wonderful big double bed and fell asleep feeling like a queen.

It was the beginning of the best four weeks of my life. The days glided by in a heady surge of pleasure, and I felt on top of the world every minute. We went to a three-star or two-star restaurant every night and had one fantastic meal after another. Then it was off to a jazz spot or disco, and a night of magical lovemaking. This time it was Steven who had to get up early for work, so he'd steal away from my room and go to his at about two A.M., and I would sleep very late and then have a light brunch at a café or the Brasserie Lipp, usually just a croissant and café au lait but sometimes also smoked salmon or berries. Then I would just walk around the entrancing city for hours, fascinated by the shops and the food stalls and the buildings and the French men and women. The weather was perfect most of the time, and on the warmest days I went sunbathing and swimming at a pool by the Seine, in just the bottom of my string bikini; toplessness was the order of the day there and it was no big thing.

It was all like a wonderful dream, and when I got back I coasted for weeks just on the memories. But the best thing of all was that it brought Steven and me back together and made us closer than ever. We've been together ever since, and he's made me very happy.

VII. The Future

So as things stand now, I'm happy with my life. Everything seems to be going well, and most of my little projects have worked out. Mitch loved his Christmas present; he told me he studied every personal ad and had a picture of himself taken so he could write to those women who ask for a photo. He showed it to me, and he handled it very cleverly; he's seated behind his desk in his best suit, smiling at the camera with that characteristic hint of mischief, and the picture makes him look appealing and solidly affluent at the same time. He wrote forty letters, and got only three replies, but one of those turned out to be just right for him, and they've developed a nice relationship. She's a securities analyst on Wall Street, and I imagine her and Mitch having long discussions about balance sheets before jumping into bed. He sees me less often than he used to, but this is one case where I'm glad to lose a little business, and I feel very happy for him.

I'm still seeing Tony and Paul and Arnie and Jerry, my all-time regulars. And of course Kathy is still my closest friend. I introduced her to Eric and they hit it off wonderfully. Eric has become a real food fiend, and the three of us dine out often and have a great time. We haven't yet convinced Eric that he should learn some kind of real trade, but we're still working on him.

Matthew and I made good on our promises to keep in touch, exchanging Christmas cards and talking on the phone every once in a while. And we had what was to be the first annual July dinner date—at La Grenouille, yet. But it turned out to be a general disaster. It was a brutally hot and humid day, and two days before the restaurant was going to close for vacation, and the food and service were good but not as exceptional as usual. Matthew and I had been expecting a warm and nostalgic time, kind of a commemoration of our summer together, but it turned out we had very little to say to each other and we both felt faintly uncomfortable. We decided it had indeed been, as they say, just one of those things, and that it was foolish to try to maintain a partial friendship and a once-a-year dinner date. So we said a very final, still civilized, good-bye, and that was that.

The big question in my life, of course, is how much longer I'm going to be a part-time call girl. And the answer is, I really don't know. Right now I'm just glad to have it and to be happy, and I don't think much about the future or worry about it. I don't want to do this all my life, of course, so I guess I'll give it another three or four years and try to save as much as I can—maybe about fifty thousand dollars, if I can slow my spending down a little—and then get married and have kids. Once in a while I toy with the idea of becoming a teacher, but I suspect I'm good at it only in a one-to-one situation, and I really don't have the ambition to go back to school and study for it.

I do definitely want to get married someday, because I don't want to be alone my whole life, but deciding that is one thing and finding the right guy is another. And if there's one thing I've learned from experience, it's that you've got to be very, very careful in choosing someone for a long-term relationship. Steven would be great in a lot of ways, and I often find myself wishing he'd settle down a little and get rid of his other women and really make a commitment to me. He might one day, when he gets a little older, but then maybe he won't seem as exciting. Who knows? My philosophy is to enjoy the present and just see what happens.

But I will retire from my part-time career someday. And at that point marriage is definitely in the cards. After all, as I always say, I'll try anything once.